Pat.

Thank you so much for your
time spent as my Deputy
Commissioner.

Ann McEachron

CELEBRATION
75 Years of Challenge and Change

CELEBRATION

75 Years of Challenge and Change

Marita Robinson

Girl Guides Guides
of Canada du Canada

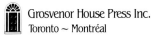
Grosvenor House Press Inc.
Toronto ~ Montréal

This book has been made possible through the generous support of Christie Brown & Co.

Copyright © by Marita Robinson, 1984

Canadian Cataloguing in Publication Data
Robinson, Marita Irenee Ensio, 1941–
    Celebration : 75 years of challenge and change

Bibliography: p.
ISBN 0-919959-05-9

1. Girl Guides of Canada — History.
I. Title.

HS3365.C3R62 1984   369.46'3'0971   C84-098659-9

Published by
Grosvenor House Press Inc., Toronto/Montréal
75 Sherbourne Street
Toronto, Ontario
M5A 2P9

Éditions Grosvenor Inc.
1456 rue Sherbrooke ouest
3ᶜ étage
Montréal, Québec
H3G 1K4

and

Girl Guides of Canada–Guides du Canada
National Headquarters
50 Merton Street
Toronto, Ontario
M4S 1A3

Printed and bound in Canada

ISBN 0 919959 05 9

Contents

Acknowledgements

Thanks to all the Provincial Councils of Guiding across Canada for their interest in and support of this anniversary project; to the late Lord and Lady Baden-Powell and Agnes Baden-Powell for their idealism and faith in youth; to the Honourable Betty Clay for her inspiration and her continuing enthusiasm for her father's work; to the writers of the excellent provincial histories of Guiding in Canada; to the many women I interviewed and to all those I could not, but would have liked to; to all those women whose lives and words are not here recorded, but who have been and are important to the success and growth of Guiding in Canada; to the staff and volunteers of the Girl Guides of Canada–Guides du Canada, National Headquarters, for their unwavering confidence in a new "sister".

Thanks for visual material in this book must go to the many Guiding members across Canada who have sent material to National Headquarters over the past three years; to various newspapers for permission to publish selected photographs; to National Archives staff member Jean Devey, former National Archivist, the late Dorothy Sellery, and current National Archivist Nancy Robinson, who, with great patience, suffered frequent raiding of their files; to National Librarian Bea Clappison for her research assistance; to Public Relations Administrators Helen Kubbinga, of National, and Jeanne Dobson, on Ontario Council, for their consistent good humour; to Marika for keeping my daily office life in order while I disappeared to write this book.

M.R.
Toronto
April 1984

PHOTOCREDITS

CHAPTER 1

Page 3 (Right), Joan Gunn;
Page 12, Mississauga News;
Page 14, Howard Anderson
Photography.

CHAPTER 2

Page 25, Canadian Champion, Milton, Ontario;
Page 27, Willey & Clarke Guelph, Ontario;
Page 34, Ministry of Education, Ontario;
Page 35; (Top), Kitchener-Waterloo Record;
Page 38, Steve Behal.

CHAPTER 3

Page 40, Vancouver Sun;
Page 52, (Bottom right), The Spectator;
Page 58, Toronto Telegram;
Page 62, Toronto Telegram.

CHAPTER 4

Page 66 (Top), Tom Bachsler, Hamilton;
Page 66 (Bottom), Calgary Herald;
Page 67 (Top), Toronto Star;
Page 74, (Below), Hamilton Spectator;
Page 74, (Right) Betty Lalonde;
Page 75, William G. Grant;
Page 86 and 87, Vancouver Province.

CHAPTER 5

Page 91, Al Popol, St. Albert–Gazette;
Page 95, Kathy Fremes.

Dedication

As Chief Commissioner of the Girl Guides of Canada – Guides du Canada, I am proud to dedicate this book to all Canadian Guiders. Throughout the development of Guiding, these women have continued to freely share their time and talents with over 275,000 young girls across Canada.

No material gesture can adequately thank Canadian Guiders for the part they have played in the growth of the Girl Guides in this country. They have made an invaluable contribution to the organization by living its philosophy and teaching its values to others. This commemorative picture book is but a small tribute to these dedicated people.

Guiding nurtures and channels resourcefulness and a generous spirit in its members. Imagination, active involvement, and love of service create the bond that unites and transcends differences. It is a bond supported by more than ideas, cemented by more than words. As our founder, Lord Baden-Powell, said, "it is recognized by deeds, not words — that is, by worthy action, not wordy faction." Such is the achievement we celebrate with this book: 75 years of challenge and change, of fun and friendship.

Canada, with its hundreds of thousands of Guides and Guiders, is part of a family of over 100 countries linked together in a sisterhood. The Girl Guides, through the Promise and the Law of Guiding, seek to help girls the world over develop into women who are valuable to their countries and to their kind.

This Canadian portrait is our contribution to the ever-growing international gallery of Guiding.

Keta E. Currah

Introduction

Cookie sales and blue or brown uniforms: that is possibly as much as many Canadians know about Girl Guiding, and for a good reason. The Girl Guides of Canada–Guides du Canada, a national organisation of over 270,000 girls and 35,000 women, has traditionally shied away from taking bows for its work in the service of the community, has sheltered its outstanding members from publicity, and has very quietly gone about its business of providing girls and women with fun, friendship, a dedication to service, and a myriad of opportunities to develop life and job skills in a nurturing and supportive environment.

Celebration: 75 Years of Challenge and Change brings the organization into the public eye. It informs readers of the basic principles of Guiding, provides a lively introduction to the history of the movement in Canada, profiles some of its finest representatives from across Canada, highlights many exciting Guiding activities from 1908 to the present, and applauds the contributions of the international Guiding sisterhood to the cause of global peace.

Celebration is a long-overdue public tribute to Guides and Guiders in Canada, and to their sisters the world over.

Karen Kain

1

Helping Girls Help Themselves

"Guiding for girls is simply a system of voluntary self-education in character, handicraft, and service for others." —*Citizenship for Girls* by Agnes Baden-Powell, 1918

(Opposite) Founder Baden-Powell talks to a Canadian Girl Guide on his first official trip to this country in 1910. (Above) Baden-Powell at a Jamboree in Budapest.

In London, England, at the Crystal Palace Boy Scout Rally in September 1909, two spunky sixteen-year-old girls, Nesta Maude Ashworth and her friend Rotha Orman, participated in women's liberation before the phrase was coined. Those early "Girl Scouts", wearing Scout hats and armed with stout broomsticks, marched proudly behind their brothers at that first Scout rally, attracting the attention of Founder Sir Robert Baden-Powell.

"As the great man came towards our little group," Nesta wrote in her memoirs, "we wondered if he would speak to us, and his opening words, so often quoted, 'What are you?' gave us the reply we were all longing to give: 'We're the Girl Scouts.' That, of course, put the ball squarely in the Chief's court and he returned it. 'You can't be; there aren't any Girl Scouts.' Back came the answer, 'Oh, yes there are, 'cos we're them!' "

Those girls were marching to make history, and they must have known it. Can't you visualize poor Sir Robert, the staunch military man, face to face with such female determination! But a good soldier knows when he is beaten, and Baden-Powell was a good soldier. Born in London, England, in 1857, Robert Baden-Powell became a world figure and a British national hero during the siege of Mafeking in the South African War of 1899–1902. Soon after distinguishing himself there, he was knighted. In 1929 he was granted a peerage by King George V. He became Lord Baden-Powell of Gilwell, the country estate given to him and to the Scout movement as a training centre after the First World War.

Besieged by strong-willed, enthusiastic "Girl Scouts", the good soldier capitulated and, two months after the Crystal Palace Boy Scout Rally, he published a pamphlet outlining the training for girls.

A few Girl Scouts who attended the first rally for Boy Scouts at the Crystal Palace, near London, on September 4, 1909. (The girls were not invited, but they begged Baden-Powell to inspect them too, and their determination helped him to change his mind and extend his training scheme to girls.)

After 1915, Rosebuds were known as Brownies, the little people of British folklore who were in the habit of doing surprise good turns.

Many of the first 6,000 members of Girl Guides were disappointed in that first training outline and unhappy about their new name and their new leader. ''Many of them,'' recalled Nesta, ''reluctantly agreed to transfer their allegiance from their self-given name of Girl Scouts, becoming instead Girl Guides.... We accepted the name,'' she continued, ''but not the fact that the Chief was no longer *our* Chief, but had handed over the leadership of the infant Organization to his sister, Miss Agnes Baden-Powell.''

What those early Guides objected to, perhaps, was being labelled ''female''. They may have been afraid that Guiding under Miss Agnes would be limited to lady-like activities of the type belonging to the tradition of Victorian upbringing for young girls. *Scouting for Boys*, that wonderful book of adventure written by Sir Robert, had drawn them to the Crystal Palace rally. This was the book, wrote Vera Armstrong in *Trefoil Tales* (1956), that they and a small number of girls like them had borrowed from their brothers, and ''in secret hiding places, poured over page by page. Whatever the boys could do, they felt they could do just as well, if not better! They could help people find their way; stop runaway horses; give first aid to the wounded; rescue people from burning houses; learn secret codes; gain badges for special achievements.'' Here they were, on the brink of a new-found freedom, on the verge of a new equality with their brothers under the leadership of ''B-P,'' as he was affectionately known, only to have their dreams squashed by the great man himself.

As it turned out, their fears that the movement would be altered for girls were well grounded, but the limitations on their activities arose not so much from Agnes Baden-Powell's pamphlets as from the objections of their own parents. Even as late as 1918, Sir Robert was having to deal with parents' notions that a girl could not be a lady and a Guide. ''Now I shall be told,'' he wrote in *Girl Guiding* (1918), ''that I am trying to make girls into tomboys. Not a bit of it—quite the opposite; but girls don't want to be dolls, they have ambitions beyond that, and also men do not desire to have dolls as their wives — they want comrades.''

Although the trappings were different, the spirit of the Guiding organization was the same as that which had engendered the Scouting movement—service for others. Both were movements founded by a man with a deep respect for, and understanding of, young people's psyches. "No one knew and understood the heart and mind of a child better than the Chief Scout," wrote future Chief Commissioner Nadine Corbett in 1941, shortly after the death of Baden-Powell. "For this reason Guiding and Scouting never go out of date. A few externals may change but the foundations are as unchanging as the girl herself."

"The spirit," said B-P, "is everything." Enthuse your girls with the spirit—once that is developed, everything comes easily; without it, success in training your girls will be practically impossible. How to do it? "Encourage a child in its natural desires, instead of instructing it in what you think it ought to do, and you can educate it on a much more solid and far-reaching basis." By giving attractive pursuits to the young, you can lead them to develop for themselves the essentials of character, health, and handiness. Study the child and see what interests her. "Develop, don't repress" her character. Above all, don't nurse her. She wants to be doing things; therefore, encourage her to do them in the right direction, and let her do them her own way. Let her make her mistakes; it is by these that she gains experience. "Education must be positive, not negative — active, not passive."

(Left) Lady Baden-Powell visits Guides in Greece, *circa* 1963. (Right) Stopover in Doe Lake, 1968. Lady Baden-Powell married more than a man; she married a movement and continued to love and to serve it as Chief Scout after her husband's death in 1941.

(Right) Early Guides camping, *circa* 1915. (Below) Nesta Maude Ashworth, Crystal Palace Guide continued to serve the Guiding organization after moving to British Columbia, Canada, *circa* 1968.

This kind of education was apparently not being provided by schools in 1909; in fact, many schools today do not seem to have the time to provide it. "The remedy largely needed," wrote B-P, "is formation of character. Character is formed more by the environment outside the school walls than by the instruction within them; that environment may be for good and at the same time it may very easily be for bad." Guiding provides the good alternative. As Aline S. Williams of Madras, India, put it in the March 1939 issue of the *Canadian Guider*: "Guiding is one of the rare influences for good which is demanded by the child herself, and we can only hope that this demand will be fully met, and that there will be no lack of capable leaders."

"Help the girls of today and we have helped the women of tomorrow," wrote Bertha Price, Captain of the First Company of Sherbrooke Girl Guides, in 1914. Sixty-five years later, in an issue of the international Guiding publication *Council Fire*, Roza de Ruffo of Peru echoed her words:

"The aim of our movement is to prepare today's girl to be tomorrow's woman."

How can an orgnization founded in and designed for the world of 1910—a world in which, as we learn from Vera Armstrong's *Trefoil Tales*, "girls wore long black stockings, skirts down to their ankles, button boots, and whenever they went out, gloves"; in which "a girl's proper place was in the home, her activities confined to needlework, music, and the arts"; in which "to be *ladylike* was the ideal"—how can such an organization work in the world of today, or of the year 2000 for that matter?

It worked yesterday, works today, and will work tomorrow because it is committed to being contemporary while holding to its great aim: "character development towards happy citizenship" in girls. The appreciation of and guidelines for developing good character are quite possibly universal, and happy citizenship can be interpreted by each country as it will. In spite of its purist aims, however, the Guiding movement did have its early detractors.

In the Victorian world, Guiding, which encouraged a girl to think for herself, to be prepared for effective action in all circumstances, and to develop a love for camping and the outdoors, was considered eccentric by some, and by a few to be an organization no nice girl would join. The mistaken impressions of those who felt it was "boy-like" and "unsexing" for girls to go out Scouting were soon clarified by a pamphlet from Headquarters in London, England, assuring them that girls did not, in fact, Scout. "This movement," the pamphlet read, "is not connected with the so-called Girl Scouts, nor is it an imitation of the Boy Scout movement. It is a purely womanly scheme and the aim of the pursuits engaged in is to make girls better housekeepers, more capable in womanly arts, from cooking to washing and sick-nursing to the training and management of children. Girls are encouraged in every way to practise the most useful subjects a woman can know so that they may become 'better mothers and guides to the next generation.' "

But the girls did camp out, of course. In fact, camping out was for Girl Guides, as for Boy Scouts, a key activity for character development. As Agnes Baden-Powell wrote in her *Handbook for Girl Guides*, "Camping out is a useful training which appeals to the girl, and is the opportunity to reach her self-reliance and resourcefulness, besides giving her health and development."

Although house-bound wives and mothers were the rule of the day, Guiding took the working world into consideration as a possible alternative for the Guide grown to womanhood. We know from Agnes Baden-Powell's *Handbook* that employment was a possibility for the early Guide at some point in her life. "Supposing that you had a fancy to have a lot of money (and it is not a thing to be sneezed at), or if you had to earn your own livelihood, there are ways you could get it," wrote Miss Baden-Powell, "provided your head is screwed on the right way." She went on to give examples of women working: nurses, teachers, typists, hairdressers, dental assistants, librarians, translators, architects, fire chiefs, and doctors. This sense of the future has always been an essential element in Guiding. Growth and change have been, and continue to be, achieved by evolution rather than revolution.

(Top) By the trail, Sardis, B.C., *circa* 1910. (Middle) Early Guides, *circa* 1910. (Bottom) Camping in New Brunswick, 1921.

After the First World War, Guides, Guiders, and women in general, having distinguished themselves in service for their countries both at home and abroad, acquired new respect in the eyes of the world. Sir Robert, taking his cue from history, produced *Girl Guiding*, a new handbook for girls in which he paid tribute to women's contributions during the war. "It was," he wrote, "a splendid exhibition of what women could do. Woman, as they say, 'came into her own,' and what was especially creditable, she came in on her own merits." He went on to encourage women to make even greater gains for their sex: "If she is to be equally efficient with her brothers for work in the world, a woman must be given equal chances with him; equal chances for picking up character and skill, discipline and bodily health, and equal chances for using them when she has got them."

In 1918 the Founder had a 1980s mentality. The cry for women's liberation came not from the radical fringe but from the heart of society. Baden-Powell still felt that a woman should experience, above all, the joys of home and family, but he was no doubt proud to admit that his Girl Guides could be every bit as responsible and resourceful as his Boy Scouts. It was not, of course, his personal discovery; it was the world's discovery. It may even have been the discovery of some of those early detractors of Guiding who had limited their daughters to lady-like existences.

Naturally, the war did not suddenly change the role of women in society, but perhaps it did give some parents second thoughts about the Guiding movement and how it could help their girls to help themselves.

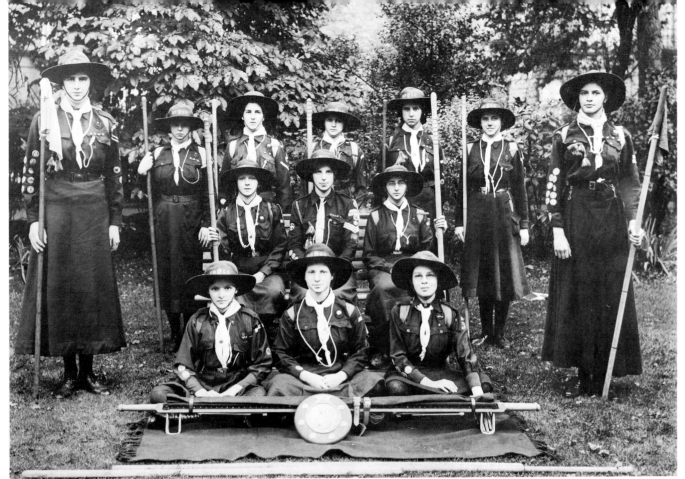

First Toronto Company, *circa* 1911-12.

Inspired by the Scouting movement, pioneer Guiders broke new ground for women the world over. Guiding companies popped up everywhere in Canada almost from the moment Boy Scout troops appeared in 1909 and, like Topsy, the movement "just growed".

Amy Leigh, active in Guiding from 1913 to 1927, started the first Guide company in Burnaby, British Columbia, at the age of fifteen.

"We even learned how to fell trees," she reports, "the very spindly little bits that would do for ridge poles for tents and that sort of thing. We took pride in felling these toothpicks just exactly where we wanted them to fall. As I look back, we were very fortunate not to have had more accidents because it was the kind of rough camping that would make any camp adviser today just cringe. We'd go down the trail to the beach. It was nothing to meet a bear! No swimming restrictions. No rules for anything! Nearest doctor twenty-five miles away. No telephones! Of course we had our own rules, which we took from *Scouting for Boys* and which we strictly adhered to, but I certainly wouldn't advocate it. It wasn't the best thing in the world. Still, it did develop self-reliance, and somehow or other we got through with it."

"I started my Guiding life," recalls Mary McDougal, a pioneer of Canadian Guiding, "by playing a game with my three little boy cousins. We were given the book *Scouting for Boys* by an English girl who had come out, and we went over to the Royal Military Grounds where the boys lived, and we played all over the grounds, exactly like we thought the Scouts should do. We lit fires, we tied our knots, we went looking for nature study. I even had a bugle to blow when we marched up and down.

"We were given khaki shirts and hats by the father of one of the boys. He had been a former Scoutmaster. We were encouraged, but we weren't registered or anything, of course. And we made paper badges, *first-class* paper badges, and we had been given cheesecloth scarves that we tied around our necks. And of course, we had our whistles, whistles belonging to the father of one of the boys. We really had fun! That was the way Guiding should be!"

The freedom, the individuality, the sense of accomplishment—these are the elements of the programme that Guides and Guiders remember and that never change.

Pathfinder's sash with emblems, 1984.

At the beginning of the Great Depression, Monica Storrs, daughter of the dean of Rochester Cathedral in England, packed her bags to embark on a wilderness life as a Sunday-school teacher in British Columbia's Peace River Country. At forty-one years old, she was following a family tradition of seeking missionary work in rough and alien surroundings. She took along her love and experience of Guiding, and through her letters to family and friends she related with warmth and humour the hardships and happy moments of her life as a pioneer teacher and Guider.

January 19, 1930: "Would you believe it—no badges have come yet for either Scouts or Guides, although all were ordered at the beginning of November. It does make it hard to keep the zest going when both Headquarters are so dilatory that I cannot get a single Guide or Scout, or even the Scout Master, enrolled."

February 1, 1930: "We are still waiting for their badges to come, and our patience is fast becoming the patience of despair."

February 22, 1930: "Thursday was Guides as usual and very much as usual, except that we are getting unusually desperate about the badges that haven't come yet."

The badges finally came, and five Guides were enrolled. "I tried," wrote Monica, "to make it an impressive and moving little ceremony, but this is very difficult with these children. It's not that they're irreverent or have mischievous humour. But they do seem to have a certain stolid matter-of-factness which it's very hard to fire with any sort of emotion or solemnity."

Monica and the girls had "a few serious differences of opinion" over the rules for bed-making for the Second-Class Badge "the two principle ones being: whether the pillows should go outside or underneath the counterpane (they all held the former as more pretty, but I got my way in the end—at least in theory) and how often you should strip the bed. The general opinion was that to do it every day (as in England) is morbid, if not hysterical. Here we arrived at a compromise of at least twice a week."

Monica, affectionately known by the inhabitants of Peace River Country as the Companion of the Peace and God's Galloping Girl, was truly a remarkable pioneer of Guiding in Canada, and she loved every wild moment of it.

In Guiding the programme is built around the girl, not the girl around the programme. Operation Outlook, Northwest Territories.

"I took the Rules of Health with the six Senior Guides," she wrote at one point, "and had the funniest discussion because they were so ingenious in explaining to me how in Canada it is impossible to keep any of them! The climax arose over teeth. I gave them a very impressive little account of germs in the mouth, and what they do, not only destroying the teeth, but poisoning the system, etc. At the end, there was a little pause and the Senior Patrol Leader remarked: 'That's funny because my father has perfect teeth and excellent health, and he has never cleaned his teeth in his life, but always laughs at us for doing it.'"

At the next meeting, Monica wrote, "we revised the Rules of Health and tried to sift through all the reasons why none of them could possibly be kept out here."

That's Guide learning as it should be—an interchange of ideas, individualism, and adapting to realities.

"The thing that intrigued me most about Guiding all along," says Betty Russell, chief of the Volunteer Bureau for the West Island of Montreal and a former active member of Guiding, "was that it was a way of having women show what they could do and do it. At first B-P didn't want the girls, but when he did decide it was a good thing, he really gave them an opportunity to do things they'd never done before. One could almost say it was a step up for women's liberation. Until then all they'd done was be good housewives—which is good, he never knocked that; you worked your way around the house and the kitchen and so on in the programme. But what man or woman in those days suggested that a girl should go skin a rabbit or catch a horse? Those things were all in the programme."

In those early years, it was pretty much every Guider for herself.

(Top) Toronto Girl Guides at Casa Loma, Toronto, March 1913. (Middle) Opening of the Girl Guide room at Casa Loma, Toronto, May 9, 1973. (Bottom) Chief Commissioner's Warrant issued to Lady Pellatt, July 24, 1912. (Opposite) Portrait of a Ranger.

"We had very little contact with even Vancouver," remembers Amy Leigh. "Headquarters was something very remote, some 3,000 miles away. It meant nothing to us except to get badges and get registered and a few things of that sort. At that time there were no controls, no regulations, no *Policy, Organization, and Rules* book. *POR* must have come in after 1927, my last year of active Guiding."

Phyllis Munday of Vancouver also felt the remoteness of Headquarters.

"At that time we knew nothing of Guide Headquarters in Toronto. We were quite surprised to find there were already other Guides in Canada. We weren't in touch with England, either. We didn't know anything about registering. Things just sort of happened in those days. They were not as organized as they are today."

Newfoundland Guiders were remote from Toronto for different reasons. "We came under English rule then," remembers Val Brown. "That was one of the great benefits of Confederation —that Newfoundland became part of the family of Girl Guides of Canada."

That was in 1949. The new union had its advantages, but there were problems, too.

"We had to change a lot of our thinking about Guiding. Not the essentials, of course, but we had a lot of headaches over *POR*, and uniforms and everything."

Almost from the very beginning there has been a Headquarters in Canada. In November 1911, Lady Mary Pellatt of Casa Loma established a committee to meet the ladies who had promised to form a Headquarters for Canadian Girl Guides. The first official location was 20 College Street, Toronto, and it was from here that all badges, registrations, and warrants sent from England were issued. A Dominion Council was formed August 12, 1912, and Lady Pellatt was appointed the first Chief Commissioner for Canada. By 1917 the Canadian Council of the Girl Guides Association was incorporated by an Act of Parliament.

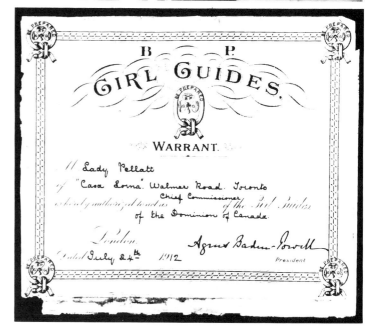

The modern Girl Guides of Canada–Guides du Canada is a volunteer organization. It is the responsibility of the paid administrative staff at provincial and national levels to execute the decisions of the volunteers who ultimately direct the various departments of the corporation and are responsible for policymaking and future planning. The Girl Guides of Canada–Guides du Canada relies on the dedication and service of over 47,000 Leaders, local association members, and Commissioners across Canada. In addition to these registered members, there are countless resource persons who make their expertise available free of charge to the Guides. Today the organization serves over 274,000 girls.

"One thing needed for success," Guider Bertha Price wrote in 1914, "is the mother's interest and co-operation." The organization has always known this, has relied on the support of parents, and has been sensitive to their direction. While Guiding has many single leaders, the majority are mothers who become involved in the organization through their daughters' participation and discover, to their delight, that Guiding is educational and fun for adults, too.

The average Guider, according to a 1982 survey by the Canadian National Headquarters, is between twenty-five and forty-four years of age, has two to three children, and is a high-school or college graduate. The story of how she came to work for the organization varies slightly from Guider to Guider, but that of Mary Jones is typical: "My thirteen-year-old daughter, Melanie, was a Pathfinder Guide, and I went along on special meetings to help. I enjoyed it! One day, the Guider-in-Charge of the unit asked me if I would be interested in taking over for her—she was getting married and leaving the city. At first I thought, no, I haven't the time; then I thought, well, yes; it would be nice to enjoy Guiding with my daughter. Then I thought, my goodness, what do I do with all those girls—I'm no teacher. I wouldn't know how to do it. Finally, I accepted the challenge."

ten is psychologically quite different from the girl of ten to fifteen."

Mary had found a fabulous book, written in 1918, called *Leaders of Girls*, by Claire Ewing Espey. She discovered that the twelve- to fifteen-year-old girl of 1984 is no different psychologically from her sister of the early 1900s. She still craves recognition of her budding personality. She still insists she's a *person* to be consulted, rather than commanded. She is still at the "me" stage of life, the age of the awakening self, the age of daydreams and romance, the age when the emotions fluctuate and the imagination becomes very active. Her life is still "a constant contrast in moods. She still swings daily between egocentrism and sociability, selfishness and altruism, radicalism and conservatism, intensified ambition and loss of interest."

"That's Melanie," thought Mary to herself.

Mary now had basic training, an understanding of her girls, and most importantly, the Promise and Law, the foundation stones of Guiding, by heart: "I promise, on my honour, to do my best; To do my duty to God, the Queen and my country; To help other people at all times; To obey the Guide law"; "A Guide's honour is to be trusted; A Guide is loyal; A Guide is useful and helps others; A Guide is a friend to all and a sister to every Guide; A Guide is courteous; A guide

Like many women who join the Guiding organization as volunteer leaders, Mary was committed to the aim of the movement, but uncertain of her talents as a leader. Having made her decision to take on the unit, Mary was introduced to her responsibilities by the Guider who had recruited her. She bought a *POR*, the book of rules governing the organization, and a uniform. It gave her a sense of belonging, an added sense of involvement in the sisterhood of Guiding.

She knew she would be required to participate in leadership training, either in a formal or an informal way. She had her *Guider Handbook*—it told her everything she had to know and gave her programme ideas—and she knew she could always call on other Guiders or her District Commissioner

for help if she needed it. There were always seminars, conferences, and district meetings to attend when she wanted to add to her skills through training. Any books, materials, badges, pins, or other items she might need for meetings were available through the Merchandizing Centre and the provincial Badge and Insignia offices.

A week away from her first meeting, Mary was armed with basic training, a lot of spirit, and a good deal more confidence. She had read *B-P's Outlook*, the Founder's book of Scouting philosophy, and her *Guider's Handbook* inside out. She had made some mental notes on the Pathfinder-age girl, based on what she knew about her own daughter's likes and dislikes. "Your first step," B-P had said, "is to study the girl herself. . . . The girl of eight to

is kind to animals and enjoys the beauty in nature; A Guide is obedient; A Guide smiles and sings even under difficulty; A Guide is thrifty; and A Guide is pure in thought, word and deed."

And it was important to keep the aim of the movement before her always, to be able to express it when parents and other interested people asked about it: "Character development towards happy citizenship. To give our girls, whatever may be their circumstances, a series of healthy and jolly activities which, while delighting them, will afford them a course of education outside the school in four particular lines." Those Mary could remember by heart: character, skills, fitness, and service for others.

"Now," she worried, "will I be able to put it all together and make it fun for the girls?"

When the night of Mary's first meeting arrived, the girls drifted in early, chatting with one another in shy tones as they entered the hall. There were eight of them finally, each an individual Mary had promised to guide into a Pathfinder world of fun and discovery over the next year.

As she greeted each girl by name, she remembered that she was not here as a teacher or an instructor but as an educator. B-P's words flashed across her mind: "Our method is to educate from within rather than to instruct from without." Our aim is to promote "not so much the acquisition of knowledge as the desire and capacity for acquiring knowledge." There was no doubt about it, she reflected, B-P was certainly influenced by the progressive educators of his day. More than once in his writings Maria Montessori was mentioned, as well as several other influential educational theorists. "The secret of the Montessori system," he had written in 1914, "is that the teacher merely organizes the work, suggests the ambition, and the boy has full liberty in accomplishing the object aimed for. . . . The Scoutmaster does not instruct, he leads the boy on to learn for himself."

13

(Top left) Girl Guide uniforms, 1963. (Bottom left) Adult uniform, 1963. (Right) Pathfinder uniform, 1979.

Mary reminded herself that she was here to inspire ambitions, to stimulate, to encourage her Pathfinders, to be not a commanding officer or a schoolmistress but an older sister. She must command the girls' respect yet still be their friend, enter into their games and laughter, win their confidence, and put herself into a position that, as B-P put it, "is essential for teaching," where by her own example she leads them in the right direction, instead of merely pointing the way.

"If it isn't fun, it isn't Guiding," Mary remembered. Thank goodness she had found time the previous night to make out those missing person cards as suggested in her *Guider Handbook*. The girls had an absolute riot of a time trying to get signatures of other girls in the unit who could "turn a cartwheel, raise one eyebrow without the other, paddle a canoe, touch their noses with their tongues," and a great long list of other talents. What a wonderful way to get to know one another. From that moment on it was a piece of cake—almost!

"Several days have passed—first meeting over," wrote a Pathfinder Leader in another part of the country. "It went well. The girls took to the idea of the Pathfinder Council, in which the entire group of girls work democratically together with interests, activities, suggestions, and discussions.

They felt that as twelve- to fifteen-year-olds they were mature and capable enough to work as a unit, discussing and evaluating their ideas, goals, and results. . . . Made a note to go over emblems, challenges, and interests this coming week. . . . Final note from last week's meeting concerns the brainstorming. Wow! The girls' ideas flew at me from all sides—involvement! Eventually we had each of the girls write down what she wanted to do this year, with her name on the paper. . . . Funny, when I think about it, ideas have been flying through my mind ever since I decided to become a Pathfinder Leader!"

There are many roads to leadership in the Guiding organization. Sometimes a woman will know a group of girls and suggest they form a unit; on other occasions, a mother or friend of the unit will take over when the Guider-in-Charge leaves the city; occasionally, girls themselves will approach a favourite person, perhaps a teacher, and ask her to form a unit and act as their Leader. In fact, forward-thinking teachers were among the earliest Guiders and schools among the earliest meeting places for Guiding units.

As a result of the rapid growth of the movement in Canada, from its earliest days the organization suffered from a lack of trained Leaders. Fortunately, however, girls were usually able to find women willing to take on the role, and before long, Guiders' training courses and training camps were set up in various provinces to ensure a continuing supply of Leaders.

Few Guiding sisters were more aware of this need than Norah C. Denny and Dorothy R. GeoHeegan, co-founders of British Columbia's famous Queen Margaret's School (QMS) in which Guiding was an integral part from the beginning. From April 1921 to February 1931, QMS Guides attended the First Cowichan Company, of which Norah and Dorothy were Guiders. "We knew," wrote Norah in *Beyond All Dreams*, "that Guiding needed leaders for the future and the fact that QMS girls were already members of our great sisterhood would make them more ready to take up work in the movement in later years."

QMS must have been a school after B-P's own heart, for as he said: "In the Scout Movement our aim is, as far as possible, so to shape our syllabus as to make it a practical form of character training, and to render it complementary to the scholastic training of the schools." He had even dared to hope, as early as 1911, that Scouting or some similar scheme "might be introduced into our continuation schools, and attendance at these be made obligatory for all boys fourteen to sixteen."

Testimonials from former staff and students at QMS illustrate the importance of Guiding principles in the school programme. Lois Godfrey was one of three sisters who attended QMS: "It meant a lot to the three of us; we had lived a sheltered life, so it taught us independence and to look after ourselves. . . . We often felt that QMS and Guiding went together."

"To me," recalls Doreen Wethy, "QMS was a wonderfully happy school, so alive, with such tremendous spirit. . . . I remember, too, the fun of Girl Guide meetings in the huts in the woods."

"Unconsciously we learned about environmental control although the phrase became popular only lately," wrote former QMS student Rosemary Owen.

(Top) Miss Norah C. Denny. (Middle) Miss Dorothy R. Geohegan. (Bottom) Katie: The School Mascot. Katie was born in 1945 in a very untidy place called "The Prefects' Study". She had full school uniform including hockey stick and pads. It should be mentioned that, in order that a record could be kept, the Captain's name tape was sewn on Katie's body and this custom remained for many years.

15

National sisterhood . . .

(Opposite, top) Provincial flags. (Opposite, bottom left) Northwest Territories. (Middle) British Columbia. (Right) Ontario.

(This page) National Sisterhood. Girl Guides' Open House, celebrating 70th Anniversary at National Headquarters, 1980. p. 27 (Bottom left) Opening of British Columbia Guide House, 1978. (Middle) Cadets of the 6th Kingston Company receiving

Gold Stage Awards of the Duke of Edinburgh. Presented on July 4, 1981, Toronto, by the Queen Mother. (Right) 1977 World Camp. Chief Commissioner Barbara Hayes and Girl Guides.

(Right) The founder, Lord Baden-Powell, on his arrival in Winnipeg, 1935. (Below) British Columbia Girl Guide Rally, Duncan, B.C., July 8, 1922. (Opposite) Brownie learns to knit.

And Anne du Moulin recalled: "For me, perhaps the most significant contribution the school made was in giving me a remarkable foretaste of freedom . . . a vivid demonstration of how women could be strong, independent, and self-assured. We were confronted with a constant demonstration that we were all capable of certain achievement, all capable of service, and all capable of realizing ourselves as complete individuals."

Serviter Fortiter ("Serve Ye Bravely") is the motto of QMS. Service takes many forms, and the training at the school was meant to continue into adult life. If citizenship can be defined as "active loyalty to the community" QMS students were good citizens in the making. QMS Guide units, like so many others across the country, served the war effort unstintingly and performed many other memorable services for their communities.

For Lord Robert Baden-Powell citizenship always meant even more than serving your community; it meant "seeing the other fellow's point of view," forgetting respective differences, and allowing the principle of brotherhood to extend its influence for good among Scouts and Guides of all nations, and through them, to people the world over. Although detractors of the movement often link it with militaristic indoctrination, Sir Robert's writings indicate that there is no indoctrination involved in the Guiding or Scouting method. The aim of the organizations is pure self-education for their members. The goal is to help children help themselves by urging them to think for themselves and to make their own decisions.

The Guide and Scout orgnizations are not "stereotyped machines bound down by rigid limitations. Some sort of order and system, of course, there must be, but the broadest principles for guidance are all that are necessary, coupled with a few minor rules to ensure fairness. In this way only can we meet the requirements of the Dominion and countries overseas to which the movement has now spread."

The flexibility that B-P built into the movement is perhaps the most difficult rule to maintain in practice, although most in the organization keep it always before them that the rules of Guiding, like the rule of any good game, allow for plenty of initiative and imagination.

B-P not only served as an inspiration, he also built a flexibile, creative organization that continues to attract leaders who strive to inspire our youth of today. "What greater thing can man achieve in this world than inspiring youth with high ideals of personal conduct?" reads a tribute to Lord Robert Baden-Powell upon his death in January 1941, in his beloved Kenya. The real tribute to B-P is that the Scouting and Guiding movements persist and are still growing. Seventy-five years after they began, they still have the flush of youth. The Guiding organization is still daring, still breaking new ground, still meeting the challenges of today's girl in her preparation to become tomorrow's woman. Baden-Powell not only knew the hearts and minds of children, and that their best education was self-education; he also knew that an organization, to be effective, to survive, has to be a growing, changing thing — has, in fact, to be creative and to constantly re-educate itself.

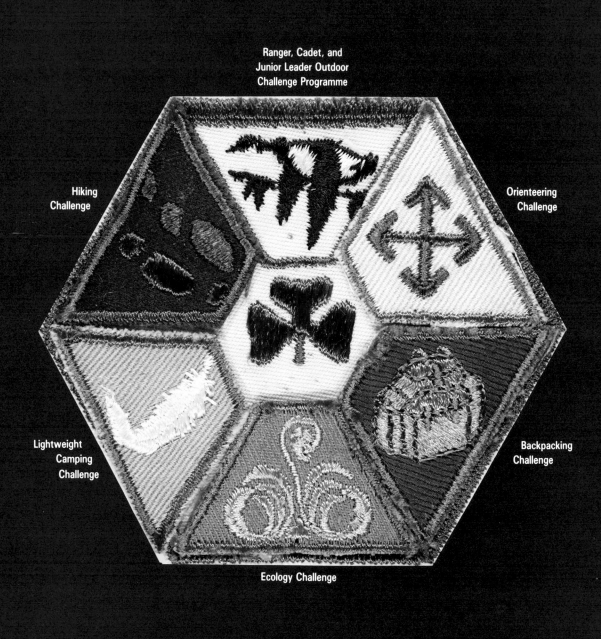

Ranger, Cadet, and
Junior Leader Outdoor
Challenge Programme

Hiking
Challenge

Orienteering
Challenge

Lightweight
Camping
Challenge

Backpacking
Challenge

Ecology Challenge

2
Adventures in Experience

"Every emblem you earn is tied up to your motto: Be Prepared."
—Juliette Low, founder of the American Girl Scouts

"I went to the Girl Guide office in London [England] the other day. It is in Victoria Street — just a step from Victoria Station. As soon as you get inside the front door you notice that everyone from the elevator boy up wears a Scout badge and all are so polite they simply fall all over themselves."

So wrote Games Mistress Marjorie Jarvis, Captain of the First Toronto Guide Company, in *The Canadian Courier* in July 1910. Miss Jarvis, a teacher at St. Mildred's School in Toronto, had gone to England on a painting scholarship from the Ontario College of Art, accompanied by Sister Barbara, Headmistress of St. Mildred's Convent School. While abroad they planned to register the school's newly formed Guide company and to pick up patrol crests and badges for the girls.

"The first thing I asked," recalled Miss Jarvis, "was: 'Do you call the people who are training the girls "Scout Mistresses"? And do you have patrols and troops?'

" 'We have patrols,' said the secretary, 'and patrol leaders the same as the boys, but three or more patrols form a company, not a troop, and the leader of it is called "Captain," and her assistant is a Lieutenant. The patrols are named after flowers, not animals—here' (showing me a large board covered with black badges, about the size of a silver dollar, each with a flower embroidered in the centre) 'are the patrol flowers, such as red roses, daisies, forget-me-nots, cornflowers, scarlet pimpernels, and so on. Each has its shoulder-knot to correspond — green and white for roses, blue for forget-me-nots, yellow and white for the daisy.'

(Right) First Aid testwork, *circa* 1931. (Below left) Julia Jarvis and her Beaver patrol meeting in Toronto, *circa* 1926. (Below right) 8th Toronto Company ''practising'', *circa* 1926.

a local committee was formed here [Toronto], as they could only be sent through a committee.''

''Really very nice'' was faint praise, and probably intended as such, for Marjorie Jarvis had been going by the book *Scouting for Boys* back home and had left younger sister Julia a happy member of a Beaver patrol.

''[Marjorie] was told that we must be called after flowers, not animals like Scouts,'' Julia wrote years later, ''it not being considered seemly for girls to go round roaring at each other like lions, or even laughing like hyenas, but that we must be gentle little flowers and just recognize each other by smell. So bang went my dear

'' 'The flowers are the Girl Guide badges, then?' I asked.

'' 'Oh, no. They are just the patrol crests — these are the badges — see, a shamrock instead of a fleur-de-lis for the Tenderfoot, and these nice embroidered ones for the Second Class and First Class Guides — the First Class with Be Prepared on it — our motto too!'

''They were really very nice; I had got the patrol crests for my company of the Toronto Girl Guides and wanted to bring these badges home for them too, but found that I had to wait till

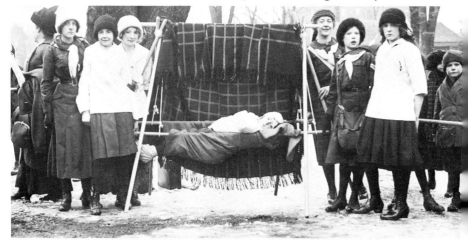

22

Beavers (slapping their tails!), and my patrol turned into Scarlet Pimpernels, which was at least romantic."

"Another basic change," wrote Julia, "was that we were to sing, not whistle, in all difficulties. This was actually a relief, as none of us could whistle, anyway; whereas any fool can sing, and most of them do."

Eager to learn just how different the Girl Guides were to be, Marjorie Jarvis continued her questions to the secretary at Headquarters in London. On the subject of tests, she discovered that a Tenderfoot Guide "has to be able to tie three knots, know the composition of the Union Jack and the Scout Law, which is practically the same for girls, only they are not bound to whistle when things go wrong. A Second-Class Guide has to cut and sew a Union Jack, lay and light a fire, make a bed, and tie six knots.

"A First-Class Guide must have one shilling in the bank, cook a simple dish, know first-aid bandaging, know simple hospital nursing, know the history of a place and be able to act as a guide to visitors, and know the whereabouts of ambulance, police, fire, and telephone stations; and bring in a Tenderfoot trained by herself, if required.

"After passing these tests girls can get efficiency badges, of which there are twenty-two."

"We have been criticized in the Scout movement," Sir Robert Baden-Powell wrote in 1916, "for offering such a large number of badges for proficiency in so many different lines. The object of this was not that each boy should try to win all these badges, but to try to meet the enormous variety of character among boys, and to give each one his chance by selecting his own subject. We do not perpetuate the school custom, whereby abilities may be equally good but, unfortunately, not in one of the subjects which come under the school curriculum."

Majorie Jarvis went on to mention "only a few" of the badges offered Girl Guides in 1910: "Ambulance, Naturalist, Cook, Musician, Gymnast, Needlewoman, Clerk, Interpreter, Signaller, Nurse, Laundress. Girls can also get life-saving badges and 'Badges of Merit' for good deeds; for, of course, a Girl Guide has to do her daily Good Turn."

There was in 1910 no special Guiding manual. That was to come later, in 1912, in the form of Agnes Baden-Powell's *How Girls Can Help to Build Up the Empire*. But there must have been some direction in 1909, since by 1910 there were already Guide patrol crests and badges. There were also "Pamphlets A and B," as they were called, which gave details of correct uniform, badge tests, and so on. Copies of these first appeared in Canada in 1909; they were sent directly by Sir Robert to Canada's first Scoutmaster, Harris Neelon of St. Catharines, Ontario. Harris gave them to a daughter of a friend who, in turn, showed them to Mary Malcolmson, who had been present at the Boy Scout Rally at Crystal Palace and who has been credited with having the first "registered" Guide company in Canada.

(Right) A Brownie's good turn. (Below) Coming soon: A Computer Badge!

Brownie's adventure. (Below) Brownie semaphore work.

"Pamphlet B," wrote Nesta Ashworth in her memoirs, "opens with the following words: 'Girls, imagine a battle has taken place in your village. Are you going to wring your hands and cry, or are you going to be brave and go out and help your fathers and brothers who are falling for you?' Then we were shown the importance of tracking and first aid to enable us to search out and bring in the wounded, signalling so we could call up the doctor, and cooking in order that we could make stews or poultices for the injured! Since the Chief Scout had always been very careful to avoid any suggestion of militarism in Scouts' training, many of the original Girl Scouts were frankly horrified. The wording, too, was over the head of the average eleven-year-old. Rotha and I had to explain that to 'wring one's hands' had nothing to do with the mangle they no doubt all had to turn on washing days! Could one really expect small Guides to bring wounded Guardsmen to safety? And supposing the doctor couldn't read Morse code? And we enjoyed the idea of poultices being included in the cook's badge!"

Of Agnes Baden-Powell's 1912 book for the daughters of the Empire, Nesta wrote: "I fear [it] was never taken very seriously as a training manual, and most Scouts and early Guiders relied on *Scouting for Boys* for training and campfire yarns." Significantly, B-P's own manual, *Girl Guiding* (1918), did not treat the war theme.

Today's manuals still abound with tests, badges, and crests, but things have definitely changed. Julia Jarvis could belong to her dear Beaver patrol now. There are blank black patrol crests available; you can be whatever you want to be. Many new badges have been added, too. In 1912 they reflected the times, as they would have in 1890 and as they do in 1984.

According to an article in the Guide magazine *Alive* (1967), "If there'd been Girl Guides in the last century, they might have worked for these badges: Salt Grater (salt came in big chunks then and had to be grated down); Knife Cleaner (there was no such thing as 'stainless steel,' so knife blades took a lot of cleaning); Boot Black (imagine cleaning all those high-button ladies' boots every day!); Berry Picker (wild berries had to be picked in season and preserved for winter use); and Rag Collector (old rags were torn up to make braided rugs). Those were some of the household chores delegated to children in the old days."

25

(Left) Aircraft Badge.

A good many of the pioneers in Guiding would be proud of the way the organization has changed with the times. The principles do not change; they will always remain the ideals for which Guides strive. But the trappings change to suit the character and needs of the modern girl. This is exactly as Baden-Powell meant it to be.

Today Brownies can earn any of over forty-three interest badges, ranging from the traditional Cook, Musician, Needleworker, and Interpreter, to Puppeteer, Explorer, and Space badges; Guides can earn any of ninety-nine interest badges, including Ecologist, Fisherman, Industrialist, Metalworker, and Weatherman. In addition to the interest badges, Brownies and Guides

(Left) Brownies, Guides, and Rangers were allowed to use the "wheelchair" display provided by the March of Dimes at a local shopping mall.

The difficulties the girls experienced in manoeuvring the wheelchairs up and down ramps and through other everyday activities made them acutely aware of the problems of the disabled. (Below) The girls then decided to hold a campfire, a most usual event for Guiding people but, as shown here, under unusual conditions.

work towards Brownie Wings and the All-Round Cord, respectively. Before she can earn her Wings, a Brownie must earn the Golden Bar, the Golden Ladder, and the Golden Hand. The programme for achieving these wings relates to the Four Pathways of Guiding: Camping and the Outdoors, Home, Community, and the World. The girl works on projects relating to the Four Pathways to make certain that she is exposed to a variety of experiences. The Wings indicate that a Brownie has done some service at home and in her community, has acquired a number of skills, and has developed a certain measure of dependability, resourcefulness, and self-reliance. The objectives are the same for each of the four Guiding branches, but the methods vary according to the ages of the girls, taking into account their particular levels of social, emotional, and physical maturity. The Four Pathways cover virtually every area of life skills. Any new badge devised by Youth Services can be fitted into an existing Pathway.

The Golden Bar and the Golden Hand of the Brownie programme become the Adventure and Voyageur Challenges of the Guide programme, representing similar but more advanced work accomplished in the Four Pathways. The Guide with an All-Round Cord has completed the Adventure and Voyageur Challenges; holds eleven specified badges; has learned about three agencies or organizations that help others and how she might contribute to work for them; has accomplished a service project; has learned about Pathfinder Guides; and has done a project showing what the Promise and Law mean to her. A lot of learning and earning—but all of it a girl's own choice. She doesn't have to earn badges to be a Guide; rather, as a Guide, she *can* earn badges.

The Pathfinder Guide earns emblems in the Four Pathway areas. Each emblem must be earned in three stages—bronze, silver, and gold. At each stage, the Pathfinder must complete ten new challenges, so that when she finally achieves her gold stage, she will have completed thirty challenges relating to the chosen emblem.

For example, a Pathfinder working towards the Camping Emblem might begin by selecting the following challenges: make a set of cookware from tin cans or demonstrate skill in the care and use of a saw, a knife, an axe, or a hatchet. The first five challenges for the bronze stage are compulsory and have to do with basic survival skills, such as knowing how to preserve food in all types of weather and how to keep it animal-proof; demonstrating how to pitch and strike a tent; knowing how to care for tents in all types of weather; and knowing what emergency equipment is necessary to carry and how to use it. Silver and gold stages are to be done on an actual campsite. As the girl progresses towards her gold stage of an emblem, she becomes a more and more knowledgeable camper.

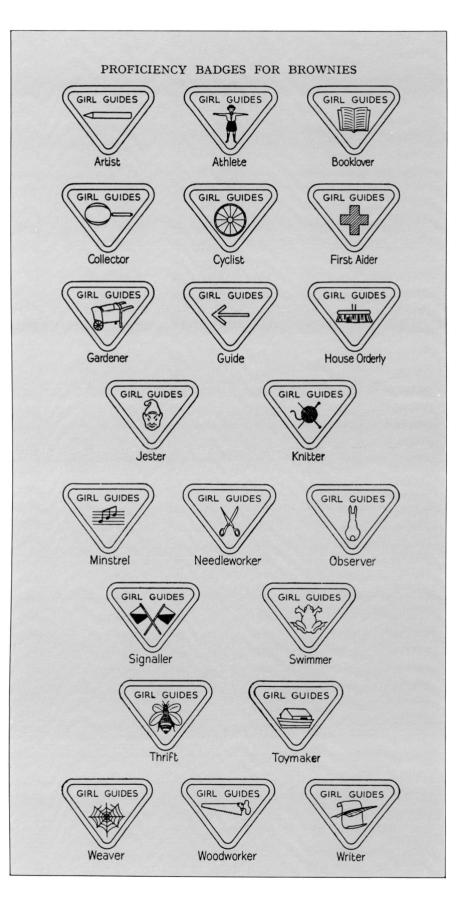

PROFICIENCY BADGES FOR BROWNIES

Artist · Athlete · Booklover
Collector · Cyclist · First Aider
Gardener · Guide · House Orderly
Jester · Knitter
Minstrel · Needleworker · Observer
Signaller · Swimmer
Thrift · Toymaker
Weaver · Woodworker · Writer

(Top) The Silver Fish Award was the highest honour to which a Guide could aspire in 1918. (Below) Winter camping is a breeze with outdoor survival skills learned in Guiding.

The highest recognition of achievement a Pathfinder can earn is the Canada Cord. For this she must have completed the three stages (bronze, silver, and gold) in each of the Four Pathways. Any registered member of a Pathfinder unit may earn the Canada Cord.

In his 1918 manual *Girl Guiding*, Sir Robert introduced the Silver Fish Award with the following observations: ''In Japan, when a child is born, a sign is hung outside the house to inform the neighbours whether it is a boy or a girl. In the case of it being a girl a doll is hoisted, while in the case of a boy a fish is displayed; the meaning being that the girl is really a plaything to look pretty, whereas the boy, like a fish, has to swim his way against the tide through life.... In the Guide movement we don't agree with this Japanese idea, and for that reason the badge of the Silver Fish is the highest honour a Guide can win, being a token and award for efficiency and ability in the girl to make her way against the tide of difficulties.''

Although it began as an award for Guides, the Silver Fish eventually became an adult award, reserved for women who had given extraordinary service to Guiding. It was a British award, and only a very few women in Canada hold it. In 1981 the National Council of the Girl Guides of Canada–Guides du Canada, decided that there was no longer any sense in having to apply to Britain each time it wished to present an award for exceptional service and so created its own gold Maple Leaf Award. This award can be given by National Council to any member of the Guiding organization who has given exceptional service, at a national level, that has contributed to the enrichment of Guiding in Canada.

In Savannah, Georgia, March 1912, Juliette Gordon Low (Daisy) formed the first troop of American Girl Guides.

Guide Music

Guide Theatre

Guide Folklore

Badges and awards are constantly reviewed and altered, cancelled, or supplemented over time to reflect changes in symbolism, technology, and programme. In a sense the badges are part of the public face of Guiding; today, for example, someone may look at the rows of them on a Guide's sleeve, pick out Ecology, and immediately determine that the organization has kept up with the times. "You wear the emblem," said Juliette Low, the founder of Girl Scouts in the United States, "to let people know that you are prepared and willing to be called on because you are a Girl Guide."

Badges, crests, emblems, and awards are a challenging part of the Guiding programme. People enjoy collecting; it has probably been a popular activity from the very earliest days of the human race. Why has there been such controversy over the years on the question of badges in the Guiding movement? Why would some Guiders happily see the badges disappear from the programme, while others feel that they are an important element that must be retained? One answer might be that there has always been controversy in Guiding. That is why it is still alive and well and on the move today. It keeps a constant check on its own fitness for the times.

Baden-Powell wrote a good deal about badges as a result of the differences of opinion that seemed to plague the subject. Scouters and Guiders of 1920 read the following: "The badges are merely intended as an encouragement to a boy to take up a hobby or occupation and to make some sort of progress in it; they are a sign to an outsider that he has done so; they are not intended to signify that he is a master in the craft which he is tested in. Therefore, the examiners should not aim at too high a standard, especially in the first badge. . . . The object is to get all boys interested, and every boy started on one or two hobbies so that he may eventually find that which suits him the best and which may offer him a career for life."

"It's perfect, really," comments Betty Russell. "That's really what it should be. As a Guider I always had a very soft spot for those who didn't bother with badges. But they still learned things."

"Badges were fun," recalls former Guide and current Brownie Guider Pat Lepper. "I remember being very proud of seeing the different colours on my badge scarf. There was no feeling of competition that I can remember. It was a personal thing, something you worked on if you wanted to. Some-

times we worked on them as a group, not really to get a badge, but to work on and learn something new. For example, we all took a St. John's Ambulance Course. It wasn't to get a badge, but to become fluent in First Aid. I don't remember people competing against one another.

"I think badges are an essential of the Guiding philosophy, which is to give young women a chance to explore themselves, to explore ideas, to learn how to fend for themselves. Badges seem to work towards that. In Brownies it's tough, of course, because you're working with very young girls who really can't go out and be astronauts right away, but you can instil some of that type of idea in them — that no doors are closed!"

Pat is a member of a Guiding family that fosters this principle. She is one of three daughters of Bernice Lepper, all of whom have been Guides and/or Leaders over the years. "Mother," says Pat, "has been in Guiding *forever*!"

Two of three Lepper girls chose non-traditional careers: the youngest, Pat, is one of two female metallurgical engineers at Algoma Steel in Sault Ste. Marie, Ontario; middle sister, Peggy, is a wood scientist with the firm of Morrison-Herschfield in Toronto,

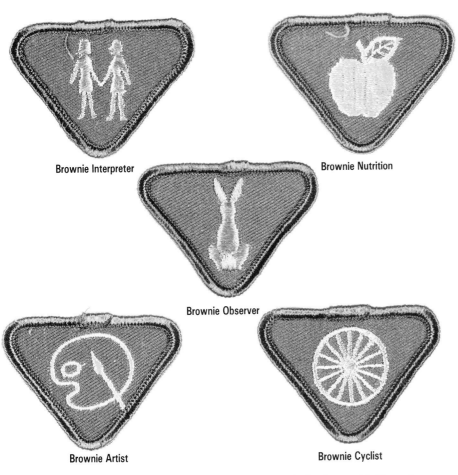

Brownie Interpreter

Brownie Nutrition

Brownie Observer

Brownie Artist

Brownie Cyclist

Guide Handywoman

Guide Athlete

Guide Ecologist

Ontario; eldest daughter, Cathy, is a Physical Education teacher at Havergal College.

"I've had such a different life from my mother," says Pat, "that it wouldn't seem logical for her to have encouraged me to pursue a completely different lifestyle from her own unless she had seen doors opening for other people, or she had been picking up philosophy that suggested anything you do is all right as long as you are proud of it and enjoy it."

As a Brown Owl Pat passes along this kind of encouragement to the young girls in her Pack: "Guiding starts by getting girls out of the home one night a week, and exposing them to lifestyles possibly different from their own. I live in a community of many ethnic groups in Sault Ste. Marie, a very tradition-minded area where the women all stay home and work and the men all go to work at plants. I'm not trying to change anyone but to give them an idea that that's not the way it has to be unless you want it to be that way. It's up to Guiders to open girls' minds to new possibilities, and I think that they can do this, just by following the programme."

"Through the fun and jollity of Scouting," said B-P, the girl is led "naturally" and "unconsciously, to develop for herself the knowledge." The badges must not become an end in themselves, so tied to the programme that the atmosphere of a meeting becomes school-like. "But if once we make it into a formal scheme of serious instruction for efficiency, we miss the whole point and value of the Scout training," wrote B-P, "and we trench on the work of the schools without the trained experts for carrying it out."

Much of the value of the Guiding programme must lie in its potential to inspire young people to explore themselves and their world, rather than to become experts at an early age. The aim is not to pass tough examinations, not to *prove* anything to anyone else, but to embark on an adventure of discovery—a new one at every turn—and to be rewarded with a personal sense of accomplishment, only occasionally connected to a badge. Adventure, Challenge, and Discovery: these are words the Guiding organization consistently uses to describe its programme.

31

The Brownie promises to do her best, to do her duty to God and to her country, and to help others. (Opposite page) The Guiding programme inspires girls of all ages and abilities to explore themselves and their world. "Let's Explore Camp," 1956. (Inset) Archer at Doe Lake, *circa* 1950.

Although Guiding has been called a movement for the middle class, Sir Robert didn't intend it to be. "As our movement attracts all classes (the poorest get equal chances and consideration with the more fortunate)," he wrote in January 1914, "much of the present human wastage will be turned into valuable citizenhood."

No one knows this better than the inner-city Guider who must frequently deal with children of many varied backgrounds. Division Commissioner Paula Warder, an inner-city Guider in Toronto, joined the organization as a Brownie, left as a Guide, and returned as a Leader.

"My group," says Paula, "has always been one that's reached out to handicapped children and to multicultural groups. We have a mix of girls from wealthy districts and from low-income homes from all across the city. It was three youngsters in wheelchairs who pulled us together. We looked after them totally — *together*! Baden-Powell's objectives were to give young people a sense of values, to help them grow up to be responsible, resourceful citizens of the world. By having this mixture of girls in my unit we're able to accomplish that, and a great deal more. The girls learn to care for those less fortunate, they learn to appreciate and work with sisters of other cultures, and they provide for each other a positive support system within the protected environment of the Guiding organization.

"When I first started working with these Rangers from the inner city, I discovered that some had never made so much as a cup of tea. We would go to camp, and all they knew how to make was toast. They were used to going to the store and buying french fries. So to talk about Canada's food guidelines was meaningless to them. As for clothes—they'd stand there freezing because all they had to bring were a teeshirt and holey socks with holey running shoes. So now when we go to camp we bring them warm clothes and all the things they need. Then gradually, bit by bit, they earn the money themselves through projects at Rangers to buy some of the equipment they need.

"The wealthier girls, who seem to have all the material luxuries in the world, have needs, too. They need someone to talk to because their parents aren't always there. Being able to share life experiences, to learn from each other, has been very valuable for my girls. We have a super group—they're so caring.

"We now have two retarded youngsters in our unit who are on government disability pensions and working in sheltered workshops. One of them, through activities and programmes at Rangers, has been able to get a job in a record company because we've taught her to be on time and to be friendly and open when meeting people, rather than shy and withdrawn. This same girl was a camper at Doe Lake camp for the handicapped last summer; this year she's going back. She's on full salary, and she's assisting on the campsite with the Let's Explore group. This is an example of the value of the Life Skills we tackle in Rangers."

Much of Paula's success must be attributed to the imagination and sensitivity with which she approaches the needs of her units. "This year," she explains, "we have a lot of top-notch kids who want to find things out and know how to go about it. They go after answers and then come back and share with us. Some Ranger groups I've had over the years couldn't do that; the girls didn't have the skills learned in the Patrol System."

The Patrol System and the Committee System are designed to prepare girls to give leadership, to accept responsi-

bility, and to work as members of a team. The Patrol System is used to meet many Guiding objectives—to provide girls with opportunities to make friends and have fun, to learn the importance of decision-making, and to function in small groups, for example.

"You have to start at the level of your group and build them up," says Paula. "If they aren't used to brainstorming and coming up with ideas, you have to be a catalyst and say 'Let's try these things.' Or you have to expose them to different places in the city or different kinds of recreation, introduce them to other Ranger or Pathfinder groups, travel—all sorts of activities that will stimulate their imaginations and widen their horizons. It has been my experience over the last thirteen to fifteen years of teaching that kids don't learn if you stand and lecture ('instruct' as B-P would put it). They need to learn by *doing*, and so do I."

Camping has always been, and no doubt for some time will continue to be, a very large part of the programme, perhaps for the very reason that it allows more possibilities for adventure. Yet, camping—in terms of time—makes up a really small part of the Guide's year. What does a Guider do with the rest of the year to make an exciting environment for her girls? How does she compete with television, video games, movies, computers, and all the activities that are commonplace in a young girl's life today?

Guiding still has to offer the young girl fun, above all. But there has to be more. It's still camping that motivates many girls to join the organization, but something else must be there to command their whole-hearted involvement. There's sisterhood, of course. And there's the knowledge of a protected environment where girls can try things out without being chided by boys. But these factors in themselves are not enough.

Technology has changed expectations for all of us, including children. The information revolution has made it possible for all of us to know an enormous amount about any given subject in a relatively short space of time. We are becoming increasingly information-hungry. Consequently the challenges young girls may expect from Guiding today have quite a different complexion from those of yesterday. As Betty Russell points out, in the days when B-P suggested girls should go camping, he was in the vanguard of the women's liberation movement, and he must have known it. Today, camping is commonplace; to suggest that a woman mustn't camp would be ludicrous.

To meet the new challenges of the 1980s the Guiding organization must prepare responsibly. It is the largest organization for women and girls the world over, and as such it has tremendous potential as the means to usher its members into the future. It has always professed to give girls the tools with which to make the most of life and its opportunities, and it will continue to do so. In countries such as the United States, Guiding is already heavily involved in career training for girls. B-P would certainly have approved. The choice is still the girl's. The fun is still what keeps her in Guiding. Camping and the outdoors are still the major training ground for the great aim of character building. Girls still learn, from the time they are Brownies on, that service to fellow human beings is the most honourable end of Guiding.

But Guiding *is* different in the 1980s. Not only does the contemporary girl have more access to information and, therefore, somewhat different expectations of Guiding, but she is also changed physiologically. Girls reach puberty much earlier today, as a rule, than did their mothers or grandmothers. Mindful of all these changes, the Girl Guides altered their age structure: in 1915 Brownies were seven and a half to eleven years old and Guides eleven to fifteen. Later, Brownies were seven to ten and Guides ten to fifteen. Today, Brownies are six to

nine; Guides, nine to twelve; Pathfinders, twelve to fifteen; and Rangers, Cadets, and Junior Leaders, fifteen to seventeen.

The change was necessary in the light of current research on age groupings. Pre-teens and young teens have very different needs psychologically, emotionally, and physically. When it comes to the question of badges, one could say that the Guide (9-12) is at the tasting stage. The girl of Pathfinder age (12-15) needs more in-depth exploration of her various challenges and interests. Both stages of a girl's development are recognized in the Guiding programme today.

(Top) The Guiding programme is for girls of all ages. Brownie (right), Guide (second from right, standing), Pathfinder (kneeling), and Ranger (left). (Bottom) Learning to lead: Patrol leaders Conference at Caddy Lake, Manitoba, 1979.

(Top) Phyllis Munday, mountain climber, naturalist, and wildlife photographer, started Guides at St. James Church in Vancouver, B.C., in 1910. (Bottom) Naju Shroff, Arthur Andersen & Co., Toronto, was involved in Guiding in India and is now Auditor for the Girls Guides of Canada–Guides du Canada.

To provide in-depth education in any subject area, Guiding has always relied extensively on outside resource persons to come in and share their expertise in various fields. This service is particularly important in the 1980s when so much information is available but is either expensive or lacks the personal touch that inspires a child to want to know more.

From its very earliest days, many Guide Leaders were professional women — teachers, social workers, and naturalists like Phyllis Munday of Vancouver, who was one of Canada's best-known mountaineers. Together with her husband, Don, she conquered the highest and most difficult peaks in the Coast Range. She was the first woman to set foot on the Peak of Mount Robson, and the first woman to reach the top of Mount Geikie. She was well known for her wildlife and

Guiding challenges keep pace with increasing opportunities for women to choose non-traditional careers.

mountain photography. Phyl, as she was affectionately known, was active in many capacities from the earliest Guiding days in British Columbia. It was she who initiated Lone Guiding in that province in 1924. At the time of her death, she was Woodcraft Adviser for British Columbia.

Professional women like Phyl became involved in Guiding because it offered them a chance to use and to expand their skills. "When I think that the skills we have acquired through Guiding are skills that people go out and pay great amounts of money for," reflects social worker and Guider trainer Pat Russell, "I am astonished! People are really amazed at the calibre of training that we give and the opportunities we offer. There are countless examples of women in our organization who, because of their Guiding experience, have launched into careers as adults that they would never have dreamed of had they not had their Guide training.

"Learning about people is really

what whetted my appetite and kept me in Guiding. I started as a Guide, and as I grew older I had opportunities to work with people in a leadership capacity. I think I discovered that I had some capabilities for working with groups. I really enjoyed being a Guide Leader as a young adult. I was about seventeen or eighteen when I started working with a Guide company, and I found I really had some talent in that direction. Eventually, after I had finished my undergraduate degree, my work with Guides led me into social work at university. That's really how I got started in my career."

"Learning by doing" is the Scout / Guide axiom, and the aim of the programme is to give the girl a chance to do things she may otherwise never try.

"Scouting is positive in its attitude to the child's own powers," wrote Chief Commissioner Estelle Wishart in 1948. "It says, 'Just think of what you can do with those hands of yours, those strong limbs, that young body. You can swim and you can cycle, you

can save a life, you can milk a cow, fell a tree, make a dress, iron a shirt, pitch a tent, draw a map, paint a picture, sing a song, dance a reel. But take the trouble to do them properly. When you think you've got the knack of it, get yourself tested. Go in for a badge.' Scouting tells youngsters, 'All work is honourable! Clean the shoes, sweep the flues, dig the garden, peel potatoes, wash dishes, sweep the floor, make the beds, shine the spoons, mend the fuse, replace the washer, darn the stockings. But take the trouble to do them properly. When you think you've got the hang of it, get yourself tested. Work for a badge!'

"People who don't understand are sometimes tempted to be superior about what they call 'badge-hunting.' Badges serve a two-fold purpose. They are the means by which Guiding presents this positive attitude to the whole range of human experience. Secondly, they divide up that whole vast range of human experience into sizeable bits that the boy or girl can cope with."

"Coping" is a word that should strike a chord in this decade, when the rate of suicide among young people between the ages of ten and sixteen is accelerating annually at a truly frightening rate in Canada and no doubt in other parts of our complex modern world as well.

"Badges," says writer Mary Elizabeth Bayer, "are very superficial symbols. They're good. Kids love them. But the important thing to realize is what they symbolize—the achievement of one's personal best. The real reward is the satisfaction one feels having done that."

"I think that the badges that related to camping and the out-of-doors were especially challenging to me," recalls Pat Russell. "They taught me to be flexible, resourceful, and open to new experiences."

37

(Left) Living far from a city centre need not keep a girl from Guiding: Lones learn skills and do testwork via mail. (Below) Lone Guide Lisa Jones (right) experienced the thrill of a lifetime meeting Canada's Mount Everest conquerers at their Base Camp, 1982.

Perhaps the ultimate example of the self-educational, self-directed learning process at work in Guiding is the Lone Guide, the girl who lives too far away from an established unit to meet weekly, or even monthly. In fact, some Lones only have contact with a Guider via post; they never meet with a registered unit at all. Yet Lones earn badges and emblems, and some have even achieved the Canada Cord upon being tested by resource people in their community. "Lones," says Marion Matheson, former National Lone Adviser, "have to be self-motivated or it would never work, no matter how encouraged they were by their parents. These girls have a great self-reliance. Lynn Schidlowsky of Saskatchewan is a fine example of how much the Lone can achieve. She was the winner of the Lone Crest Design competition held by the National Office, and she has qualified, by virtue of her accomplishments in Guiding, for two international trips. Lone Cadet Lisa Jones of Nova Scotia was one of the two Guides privileged to trek to base camp at Mount Everest and meet the Canadian conquerors of the peak in 1982."

Lones rely heavily on letters mailed by Guiders to each individual girl. These letters contain personal news from members of the unit to create a sense of camaraderie and include instructions on requirements for various badges and emblems towards which girls might be working. Most of these girls do not have the fellowship of a unit meeting available to them, and thus the letters are a rather exciting item to find in the post box every month.

"British Columbia is our most active province in Lone Guiding," Marion Matheson explains, "probably because of the leadership. The Provincial Commissioner there wrote to the Department of Education to see if they had any girls in remote areas who might be interested in becoming Lone Guides. The response was tremendous. Alberta, Manitoba, and Ontario have followed B.C.'s lead. The schools have been happy for the opportunity. As you can imagine, in some of these remote areas the extracurricular activities are rather limited."

To understand where Lones began and why they're important to the future of Guiding, we have to go back to England, to a September morning in 1912, and to a telephone conversation between Nesta Maude Ashworth and Agnes Baden-Powell. At that time Nesta was twenty and had been a Guide for two years and a Scout for two before that. She had worked in the Guide Headquarters and had helped at various camps. Headquarters in London was besieged by letters from girls "saying that they wanted to be Guides but lived far away from any company and, please, would someone tell them how they could join." Nesta was called upon to deal with these persistent young people. She agreed to answer the letters and to be, in fact, the captain of the First Lone Company.

3

Adventures in Creativity

"If it isn't fun, it isn't Guiding." —Lord Robert Baden-Powell

We are all unique individuals, each our own person and creation; in our every act, therefore, we are already creative. But perhaps we long to be able to make things, to play a part, to sing with a group, to invent something, to learn photography, to paint with oils, or to be able to come up with a hundred ways to amuse ourselves on a rainy day — to have fun, to try to something we've never tried before.

Guiding helps girls to explore their own creativity. It's an adventure shared by Guides and Guiders alike, and like any adventure it is more fun if it is shared with good companions. Through fun, friendship, and games, the Guide learns to see imaginatively; she acquires and applies skills in crafts and the performing arts; and through brainstorming she learns to think creatively. Brainstorming is a quick way to get many ideas from a group. A specific topic is chosen, such as the presentation of the Brownie story in skit form for a special occasion, and members of the group are asked for ideas on this topic. Someone writes down the ideas quickly where everyone can see them. All ideas put forward are recorded without criticism. Brainstorming encourages a girl to look wide in the search for solutions to problems or possibilities for action.

When a girl is a Brownie, she might play dress-up games or mime the Brownie story; when she is a Guide, she might go on an imaginary trip around the world, encountering situations on each continent that call forth her Guiding skills; in Pathfinder Guides she might play a simulation game in which she experiences the feelings of the rich and poor in the world; and in Rangers she might help to write, direct, design, and produce a play or a puppet show. The growth in ability to plan, carry out, and perform the skills involved is evident in a girl's growth from Brownie to Ranger or Cadet. Through all the steps and stages, a girl is encouraged to create her self, as much as to create a poem, a picture, or a play. That self is the final product of her Guiding experience. From the very early days of its history, the creative programme in Guiding has included nature lore, music, dance, arts and crafts, and theatre.

Inventing skits was part of the fun of Guiding even in early times.

"Acting," Lord Baden-Powell said, "ought to form part of every boy's [and girl's] education." In coming to "know the beauties of Shakespeare and other authors, a child can feel, while expressing them, the emotions of joy and sorrow, love and sympathy." Having felt and resolved them in dramatic form, the child might then be better able to translate such feelings into art or to handle them more easily in her own life.

"Skits," reported Guider Connie Beauchamp in a 1981 issue of the *Canadian Guider*, "are probably the most frequently used form of Drama in the Guide Company, and perhaps in the Brownie Pack and Pathfinder units as well. If done well," she observed, "they can serve many purposes, besides the fun of acting them out: stimulate creativity, foster recognition of one's peers, develop teamwork, build confidence, modify undesirable behaviour, and enhance listening skills."

"Girl Guides Give Clever Play" reads a 1912 headline in the *Toronto Daily News*: "The various laws were splendidly demonstrated by clever scenes. In one outdoor scene the girls constructed a hut in the woods, made a ladder and wove a mattress. . . . A great deal of amusement was afforded in the scene illustrating Kindness to Animals, when a tame duck with the aristocratic name of Percy, a cat and a dog were on the stage."

"We invented our skits," remembers one former Guide, Montreal actress Bernice Picard, "from the activities we had during the day or from a story or a song." She recalls one in particular, the *ratatouille* sketch: "I don't know what happened; we made this *ratatouille* and it was too salty! Nobody wanted to eat it. We wanted to make people laugh, to relax about the *ratatouille*, so we started thinking up funny lines about the salt. We built a whole story around it. We had all these people tasting the stew. 'Do you mind if I salt this?' one would say. Then someone else would come along and say, 'Hey, Micheline forgot the salt.' In the end, everybody was salting the *ratatouille*."

That's not very sophisticated theatre, perhaps, but it's the creative process at work, nevertheless.

"The most fun I remember," continues Bernice, reminiscing about her Guiding days, "was at camp. I particularly remember the campfire times. There was always something of the actress in me because whenever it came to setting up song nights or sketches, I was always the first to suggest themes, to do the casting, to find the costumes. Of course, I wasn't the only enthusiastic one; there were others like me who were interested, who nevertheless did not become actresses. Still, I think Guiding did help me to explore the actress in myself."

"We have a very special tradition for campfires in Guiding," comments former National Music Adviser, Donna Haley. "Each one is really a dramatic presentation that has a definite framework — a beginning, a middle, and an end. Within that framework we seek to create a feeling of enjoyment, fun, camaraderie, and participation. It is not just a sing-song. It is not a formal theatrical production. It is not a skit or stunt night. It's a campfire."

One wonders how many future performers like Bernice Picard had their first taste of theatre at summer camp. How many earned their Entertainer's Badge, the badge that Baden-Powell himself thought so important? "I am sure," he wrote, "that it is a good thing to do a bit of play-acting when you are young. At school I was encouraged to do a lot of it and I have thanked my lucky stars ever since that I did so. For one thing, it taught me to learn yards of stuff by heart; also it accustomed me to speak clearly and without nervousness before a lot of people; and it gave me the novel joy of being someone else for a time. Above all it gave one the pleasure and happiness of giving pleasure to other people at times when they needed it."

No girl's talents are ignored when it comes to programming for campfire.

Provincial Guiding histories are full of references to theatrical performances, skits, and pageants great and small, given by Guides from one end of Canada to the other. Not only were they performed; they were most often created from scratch — words, music, song, and dance. A group of Guides from Kings County, Nova Scotia, "prepared a play for the [Christmas] season that, since it succeeded in its local presentations, they took to Halifax and performed for the little patients in the Children's Hospital."

Betty Frost, former Provincial Secretary for British Columbia, remembers: "During the time I worked in the office I was a Guider as well, and I think the times I enjoyed most were those spent preparing for our marvellous pageants that we put on every few years at the Forum. I remember so vividly one in particular, when my company was asked to put on a camping display. We were full of ideas, but how difficult to pitch a tent on a wooden floor! After hours of practice we solved our problem and were able to pitch the tent in three minutes, using two tall Guides inside as supports for the ridge pole and the smallest ones crouching down as tent pegs

with brown paper bags over their heads."

The Brandon, Manitoba, *Daily Sun* reported in 1916 that at their summer camp at Lake Clementi, the Girl Guides held a very enjoyable and successful open-air entertainment that included, among other things, "delightful dancing numbers" that "consisted of aesthetic dancing movements by Guides in Grecian costumes", a reading by Miss Lillian Edmison, a mouth-organ solo by Miss Pearl Jones, and "songs by the Guides".

Cochrane, Alberta, Guides presented a play entitled *My Aunt's Heiress* at the town hall in 1916. The show, observed a local reviewer, "was well-staged and showed that a large amount of time must have been spent to train the girls for the different parts." But it proved a touch problematic for its audience as the reviewer noted: "An amusing song, with speeches, entitled 'Suffragettes,' was rendered by the girls in fine style. It made the men very uncomfortable. One gentleman suggested that Mrs. Pankhurst was just looking for girls like the ones who made the speeches."

Two girls—Alison Cottle of Kelowna, British Columbia, and Irene La Prairie, of Sydney, British Columbia, were selected to attend the Festival of Performing Arts at Our Cabaña in Cuernavaca, Mexico, in January 1982. There they learned and practised techniques for developing and directing activities in drama, dance, and choral music. The climax of the two-week course was a stage presentation combining these three art forms.

Songs and singing have always been a part of the Girl Guide programme —such important part that each province has music advisers at several different levels. The National Music Adviser is someone who is thoroughly familiar and experienced with music at all levels of the Guiding programme and who is aware of current teaching methods and trends. She acts as a resource person for the provincial music advisers. She is responsible for any national music event. Among those held annually is the Cadet and Ranger singing competition, first held in 1974. It was won in 1983 by the First St. Andrews Rangers of Willowdale, Ontario.

Not only the younger girls sing in Guiding. The Trefoil Singers of Ontario, formed in 1950, were retired Guides and Guiders who became quite well known for their professional rendition of Guide songs and folk songs as well. As interest in the choir increased, competition in the Kiwanis Festival became a major project. For three successive years the choir won the Campfire Singing class and retained the shield permanently for their achievements.

And it's not only singing that Guides do; they are encouraged to compose their own songs as well. In 1979 a new age grouping became effective in the Girl Guide organization—the Pathfinders, for girls age twelve to fifteen. The introduction of this new Pathfinder Guides group called for celebration; in 1980, a Pathfinder Song competition, open to girls, Guiders, and even non-Guide people, was won by Marguerite Helps, of Edmonton, Alberta, a Guider of twenty years' standing. It was her very first song.

"The enjoyment of rendering or of hearing music," said Baden-Powell in 1919, "is common to all the human

Canadian Guiding publications. Since 1933, Canadian Guide Leaders have had their own national magazine, *Canadian Guider*, which serves both as a training vehicle and a pipeline from Headquarters to grass roots.

family. The song as a setting to words enables the soul to give itself expression which, when adequately done, brings pleasure both to the singer and [her] hearer.... Through [her] natural love of music, the [girl] can be linked up with poetry and higher sentiment as by a natural and easy transition. It opens a ready means to the [Guider] of teaching happiness to [her girls] and, at the same time, of raising the tone of their thoughts.''

''Through her natural love'' — that's the way Guiding works in every respect, by keeping in touch with the girls' own desires. It was with this in mind that *The Canadian Guide* magazine was launched in March of 1949. This publication, which continued until 1972, was the girls' direct pipeline to the leaders of the movement. Through *The Canadian Guide* a girl could make known her feelings about various aspects of the organization; it offered her a forum for her viewpoints and an outlet for her creative talents. The magazine ran short-story, essay, and poetry contests, open to all Guides across Canada. In the early 1950s the Walter Donald Ross photographic competition was initiated. When the money donated for this purpose ran out in 1979, Kodak Canada took over the contest, which ran every year until 1983. There were poster-design competitions, colour-slide competitions, and even a new-name-for-your-magazine contest, which changed the masthead to *Alive* in June 1966.

Even before the arrival of the national magazine, it was obvious that such a publication was necessary. In 1915, Guides of the First Burnaby Company in British Columbia, led by teenager Amy Leigh, produced and printed a paper of their own called *The Burnaby Guide Monthly*. By 1923 the First Burnaby Ranger Company was organized, again by Amy Leigh, and began to publish a company paper, *The Ranger Star*. Today, the Rangers have their own publication, *Karma*, edited by Wendy Dale, produced through National Headquarters in Toronto.

Skits, campfires, contests, their own magazine—just a few of the things that make Guiding fun. But perhaps the happiest memories of most Guides are those of camp. Creativity is apparent in Guide camps as well, with most provinces offering girls many special theme camps from which to choose each summer.

Tsoona, British Columbia, organized an Arts and Crafts Camp in 1969, for example. It offered everything from cloth draping and batik to wax carving, paper folding, guitar, and creative drama. The first Arts and Crafts Festival, according to *The Canadian Guide*, was a "special venture in international friendship" that took place at Ontario's Doe Lake Camp in the summer of 1965. Sixteen Rangers from Ontario joined twelve American Girl Scouts, two Guides from Argentina, and one from Guatemala for a week-long camp devoted to trading skills in the arts and crafts. "The Argentinian and Guatemalan girls taught the Rangers and the Girl Scouts of the U.S.A. how to do beadwork and weaving typical of the Indians of South and Central America. The Rangers, in turn, taught their guests how to carve totem poles and how to make pictures on burlap sacking material in the French-Canadian style."

(Above) Scene from a historical skit at Heritage Camp, 1967.

At the National Heritage Camp celebrating Canada's Centennial, held on Morrison and Nairn islands in the St. Lawrence River in July 1967, one of the most popular crafts taught was the ancient art of rug hooking. Within the first few hours of camp, all 140 frames were in use, and many eager girls were waiting for their turn! The crafts of Canada's Indians and Inuit and the handicrafts brought to this country by the early settlers were all represented at Heritage Camp in 1967 and continue to be taught at Guide camps across the country.

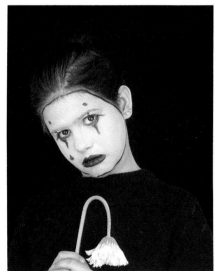

"We should be endeavouring to recognize and protect our creative heritage," wrote the Chairman of the World Association of Girl Guides / Girl Scouts in *Council Fire*, the international publication of the Guiding organization (April 1982), "to give the younger generation chances to participate in creative activities and to discover and encourage the creative heritage to be passed on to those that follow."

The arts-and-crafts programme in Guiding is all the more remarkable when one remembers that Guiders are volunteers. While it may be true that some are professional weavers, sculptors, musicians, dancers, and ceramic artists, the vast majority are dedicated women who must use their Guiding intelligence and resourcefulness either to learn the craft they wish to share with their girls or to organize professionals willing to share their talents free of charge to Guides.

For this reason, networking and talent-pooling have become an increasingly important part of Guiding over the years. Ontario, for example, has a sub-committee of twenty or more Guiders with expertise in various arts; this team travels across the province sharing its talents with other leaders. In 1982, New Brunswick training and camping Guiders got together a team of nineteen talented Guiders. "Some," says spokeswoman Ann Connolly, "were experts in special areas of

Guiding, such as advanced camping, nature, and music. Others were good at many things, but all were willing to share their knowledge with others. We divided into eight teams, each with a specific training we would be responsible for. These sessions were Basic Camping, Advanced Camping, Leadership, Wide Games [games played outdoors in large, open spaces], Nature, Music, Crafts, and Drama. A fun-filled campfire was presented at each camp, highlighted by a puppet show."

(Below) Puppet show at Doe Lake Music Camp, 1963. (Right) Trading friendship pins, Heritage Camp, 1967.

This co-operative effort is what Guiding is all about—a sharing of talents and resources in an atmosphere of fun.

"We all learned a great deal," recalls Ann, "and we sang and laughed from morning till night."

Whether it's a skit, a puppet show, a campfire, or a drawing, it must be something that is fun to do.

"I remember," wrote B-P in 1928, "how my education in Greek was a dead washout because they tried to teach me the grammar first, with all its intricacies and uninteresting detail, before showing me anything of the beauty of the language itself. In the same way," he said, " a youngster who is anxious to draw is often put off by having to go through a course of making straight lines and curves up to the required standard and drawing blocks and cubes, etc. Whereas to the young mind eager to express itself one can do better, I think, by encouraging a boy to paint a volcano in eruption, if you want to encourage his colour vision, or to draw any incident that interests him."

Drawing, B-P felt, could be used to develop observation, imagination, self-expression, a sense of beauty, and therefore a heightened form of enjoyment of life. Through drawing a child could become aware that "even in sordid surroundings there may yet be light and shadow, colour and beauty."

B-P must have been a fine example of the happy, creative character he hoped to foster in young people; he practised what he preached. His writings reveal a man who saw the sunny side of life, who could see something positive even in the most negative of situations. He appreciated humour and was himself quite an accomplished cartoonist, as drawings sprinkled throughout his books suggest. But it was more than humour that fed his cheerful disposition. He was a man who appreciated beauty and the joy that it could give.

"He was," said Lady Baden-Powell of her husband upon his death in 1941, "one of the happiest of men, and all his last messages point to his desire that we should be happy too."

His legacy to the youth of the world was his own formula for this happiness —an appreciation of life's beauties and a character predisposed to help one's fellow human beings. Both call for a creative imagination, an ability to see the unusual in the usual, an ability to step into another's shoes.

Perhaps artists, whether they do it consciously or not, allow themselves to be most open to life's hidden beauties, to the "gleams" that give joy, as B-P calls them. To a painter or a photographer, a pair of worn, unlaced boots flung onto the vast space of a cement floor in an empty firehall

A response to beauty in nature is a Guide's first step to art appreciation.

would tell a story; these elements, placed together by chance, form an exquisite moment that might move an artist to creation. A choreographer walking along a city street might be struck by people's poses, might see in them a beauty that many would not, might catch a "gleam" that, translated, becomes dance.

If you and I look at what the painter and the choreographer have created, will we see the "gleams" they saw? Probably not, but we might see the way each person translated reality into art, provided that in their translation there are familiar elements. Herein lies one definition of art: the combining of ordinary elements in a surprising, illuminating new way. B-P believed that the best way to appreciate beauty is through the study of nature.

"Nature lore," he wrote, "as I have probably insisted only too often, gives the best means of opening out the minds and thoughts of [girls]. As the wonders of Nature are unfolded to the young mind, so too its beauties can be pointed out and gradually become recognized. When appreciation of beauty is once given a place in the mind, it grows automatically in the same way as observation, and brings joy in the greyest surroundings.... When the beautiful begins to catch hold, the young mind seems to yearn to express itself in something other than everyday prose."

Two verses, one by a Nova Scotia Guider and the second by an Ontario Brownie, illustrate his point.

Look wide, to where the distant mountains raise
  Their shadowed peaks to meet the open sky;
Look far, and see the sailing ships display
  Their sails to catch the wind that passes by;
Look out, and watch the budding leaf unfold,
  And all the wonders that the spring will hold;
Look high, and try to solve the mystery
  Of that enormous, star-filled canopy.
Look round, and see how people near you fare —
  Perhaps you have some treasure they could share
To show how they could glean from Life's hard way
  These moments rare when through each busy day
You pause, to let your gaze go wand'ring wide
  In search of beauty on the countryside.

—Joan Sokoloff, Brown Owl, the Eighth
Brownie Pack, Sydney, Nova Scotia, 1936

My home is by the lake side
Where sea gulls flit and soar
Where rustling pine and cedar tall
Bend low to waves that roar.

There at night the stars look down
On a rippling world of foam
And moonlight makes a silvery path
Out to its great round home.

Not far away is a lazy creek
Spread with lilies white and gold
Where tall blue heron stand on guard
Like shepherds of the fold.

—*Annetta Conklin, Second Brownie Pack,
Kingsville, Ontario, 1949*

"Look wide!" says Guiding. "See" and "respond" says the creative personality. The poet may not be moved to poetry on the spot. She may be spellbound by the moment. But she will assimilate. She will form a memory of beauty. She will see, and what she sees may inspire a poem.

"It begins with a feeling about something that is stimulated from an unknown well inside yourself," says poet Mary Elizabeth Bayer, former Provincial Commissioner for Manitoba and a long-time member of the Guiding sisterhood. "Then there's a process of intellectualizing that goes on in the head because you're trying to express something in words. Then there's a selection of, hopefully, the most appropriate images or ideas or designs of thought to express that something in such a way that it can be communicated to the person reading it."

A common approach to the teaching of art is the study of great works by the master painters; in Guiding, it is the study of nature. The unexpected glitter of dew on a morning cobweb, the sparkle of sunlight in a stream, a mother's red-gold-hair—these are the child's best educators in art.

Through nature lore, says B-P, the girl develops the "power of appreciating beauty in Nature and, consequently, in art." It may be difficult for a young person to see beauty in a Van Gogh painting, but have her study a wheatfield in the searing sunlight, have her bask in nature's panorama, and she may sense within herself the beauty that inspired the creation of the painting, the sonata, or the poem. A painter can capture the mothering of a cub by a wolf and make us wonder at it, but nature teaches by example; it surrounds us, makes us part of the picture, allows us to *experience* beauty.

That's the difference, for B-P, between the "work of art" and "nature" as teachers of beauty. His is the notion of *art as experience*, of art as participation rather than spectacle. Having been part of the artistic landscape, he suggests, the girl can better appreciate the beauty of it and can better represent it.

53

Karen Kain dancing in *Elite Syncopations* for The National Ballet of Canada.

A principal dancer with the National Ballet of Canada, Karen Kain is an artist with a great deal of respect for the Girl Guide organization and its aim of helping girls to become happy, resourceful, and responsible individuals and citizens. She happened to be in Cape Breton on tour at the time of the International Camp in 1977 and was delighted to appear as a guest speaker.

"I certainly got a good feeling about Guiding from that camp," she said in an interview. "The girls were having a fabulous time. They were making a lot of friends from across the country and around the world. It seemed like a very healthy, wonderful way for girls to be spending a few weeks in the summer."

Although she has never been a Guide herself, Ms. Kain can appreciate B-P's comments on the study of art. "The study of art and related subjects builds a more civilized person, perhaps," she observes, "but I don't know that it necessarily makes you a better kind of person." She may not entirely agree with B-P's notion that the study of nature can ultimately create good character, but she knows what he means by "gleams".

"It's the sunshine streaming through the studio window after a class," she muses, and adds: "It's important for people to see little things like that in life and to find joy in them."

"Joy" is the operative word in character-building for the Guiding organization. Nature lore leads to an appreciation of beauty in art, and in life. With the appreciation of beauty comes joy and a sense of pleasure in both seeing and doing. Doing itself becomes more creative.

We can all experience art in B-P's terms. Best of all, of course, we find art in nature, but, in the final analysis, it is everywhere around us. He liked to think of beautiful things and exquisite moments in life as "little gleams that bring joy". He felt that those who recognize such gleams and experience the joy they bring are likely to know how to create those gleams for others. It all begins with nature lore. Nature not only moves us to see beauty but

(Left) Instructions in bicycle safety, *circa* 1965. (Below) Surrounded by a ring of Brownies, North Vancouver District Commissioner Mrs. T.R. Buckham discussed the Native Lore badge with Alice Burritt, "Life Princess of the North American Indian Brotherhood." Mrs. Burritt, whose Indian name is Princess Ame-Shun, has been most active in preserving Indian artifacts and teaching authentic history to all the local Guiding groups.

also inspires us to become better people.

While this may seem to be a rather simplistic approach to life, many would, none the less, find it commendable. B-P doesn't suggest, after all, that one can ignore suffering or misfortune but rather that in developing a positive approach to life one can seek to rise above them. Not a bad recipe for good character.

"It's very limiting to talk about artists being the creative people," comments Ruth Sheppard, President of Toastmistress International and a former Division Commissioner in the Girl Guides of Canada–Guides du Canada. "A person who is not an artist can be creative. If you have a new way of doing something—that's creative! It could be something mundane. It could be a housewife doing housework—she's found a way to do it more efficiently and more quickly—that's creativity!"

"The most important thing that Guiding did for me," says Bernice Picard, "is that it gave me the desire to improve all the time, to learn from everybody and everything around me. To hear, to see. To assimilate it all. To have it become something else in me. It gave me the desire and ability to improve constantly. It's not a question of not being satisfied with what we are, but of taking what we are further."

As Karen Kain points out: "Even people who have a special talent have to go through the self-actualization process. You can be very gifted in one area, but in other areas of your life you still need to find out who you are. Just having a wonderful voice and being able to sing—it really is a very small part of who you are and what you have to offer in your life."

Guiding, as Mary Elizabeth Bayer explains, encourages a girl to explore different avenues of her self. "Because of the variety of experiences that Guiding offers, a girl can touch on all kinds of areas of interest—the outdoors, the environment, all manner of skills she can acquire, collecting, history, and the arts—whatever it may be. All this variety is offered, and therefore the growing person is able to say, 'My gosh! The world is full of wonderful things. I think I'll choose this, this, and this out of the enormous smorgasbord that's offered.'"

55

Top international model Leslie Durnin.

Being in the Girl Guides showed nineteen-year-old Lesley Durnin that "there was a whole world out there" and encouraged her to develop her career as a model. "When I was a Brownie, and then a Ranger, I learned how to speak in front of people, not to be afraid." Lesley, a former Ottawa resident, is now a fashion model living in Milan, Italy.

In Guiding each girl achieves her maximum.

"Guiding," says Mary Elizabeth Bayer, "is carefully designed to enable people to struggle towards and reach their own level, their own limits. Competition is not such that you have to be first-class in absolutely everything. There is something for everyone in Guiding. To that extent, people are not frightened off; they are able to achieve the maximum of themselves. Then Guiding also provides a structure of appreciation and recognition of that achievement, whatever it is. A small achievement is recognized as well as a major one. And I think this is very important—to be assured, to be recognized. Guiding has both the challenge and the reward. Both are incorporated into the programme. From that point of view it's a magnificent programme for people who are eager to realize their own maximum, to achieve their personal best."

"Make yourself," B-P said. This is his call to self-actualization, to the formation of one's own character, a character that might display the following: awareness, spontaneity, adaptive flexibility, divergent thinking, openness to new experience, an ability to be born anew every day, a relish for temporary chaos, the capacity to be puzzled, and a tolerance of ambiguity.

(Far right) Three Rangers from the Toronto brigantine *Pathfinder* man the rigging while others look up from the deck. Twenty girls set out for a cruise around Lake Ontario, part of a sail-training program in preparation for a weekend trip to Niagara Falls.

Character education, such as that offered in the Girl Guide and Boy Scout organizations, was not available in schools, B-P maintained. Not in 1913, when he wrote that although the three R's were taught, character was "left for pupils to pick up for themselves out of school hours, according to their environment." Not in 1918, when he wrote: "Though it is vastly improved of late years [school] cannot under existing conditions entirely prepare the girl for what is possible for her in the present day, much less for what will be required of her in the future." And not in 1938, when he wrote: "Character training has yet to be taken up by education authorities, when they see how to teach it in a practical way, but it does more good than all the reading, writing, and arithmetic put together." The gathering war clouds prompted him to add: "This mass hypnotism, which leads to mass hysterics and mass panics, can only be overcome by training the individual to have character of his own, character to know his own mind, standing up for the right, giving real help in difficult situations."

Girls in most schools may not have been getting character training then, but girls in the Girl Guides certainly are today, as this example of giving real help in a difficult situation illustrates.

On July 17, 1967, at approximately 7:00 p.m., seventeen-year-old Ruth McWilliams, paymaster of the SRS *Micmac* Haney Sea Rangers in British Columbia, was driving to Port Coquitlam to swim. While crossing the Pitt River bridge on Highway Seven, she noticed a man rush into the water fully clothed, attempting to rescue a child. She quickly decided she might be able to help. The Pitt River is approximately 100 to 125 yards across and 60 feet deep mid-stream, with eddys and whirlpools. Often the bodies of those who drown in this river are not recovered until days or months later and then far downstream.

Ruth raced the car off the bridge 50 yards along to the dyke, slammed on the brakes, and ran along the dyke, jumping a barbed-wire fence and peeling off her outer clothes to her bathing suit underneath. She dove in and swam under a log boom and finally surfaced with the boy about 10 yards from shore. He wasn't breathing. She gave him a hard blow on the back to make him breathe but knocked him out of her grip—he immediately sank out of sight into the muddy undertow. She dove, surfaced for air, dove, surfaced, and dove for the third time; finally, he floated into her arms and they surfaced together. By this time they were under the bridge and the current forced her to carry him in a diagonal path to the Marine float many yards downstream from where the accident occurred. She literally threw the boy up onto the wharf and scrambled up after him. He was blue, not breathing. Ruth applied mouth-to-mouth resuscitation for what seemed like hours, but the boy's father said it was approximately fifteen minutes. The boy began to breathe on his own and vomited. Ruth and the father talked afterwards; in a very few minutes the boy was running around again, playing just like any child.

Montreal Sea Ranger. Circa 1960s.

Ruth was presented with the highest award for gallantry offered by the Girl Guides of Canada—the Bronze Cross. She had risked her life to save the boy. Her Sea Ranger Skipper, Joan McLennan, asked Ruth what she had been thinking during this dramatic rescue. She said, "I guess I just didn't think much about anything. If I had stopped to think of risk and danger too long, I wouldn't have been much help, would I? I did think though of my father's car. Was it stopped when I jumped out? Was the emergency brake on? If it rolled into the river he'd kill me!"

Ruth's was not a logical action. Had she thought it through, had she stopped to consider the risk to her own life, she might not have acted with such bravery. Hers was a creative response.

"A prerequisite for creativity," wrote Jeffrey Hollman in 1982 in *The English Journal*, "is the ability to produce a large number of responses to a given situation. In educational jargon this is called divergent production: 'Come up with as many answers to this question as you can.' Most of American education stresses convergent production, a process which requires the single, most right answer to a question: 'Who was the first president of the United States?'" Guiding, on the other hand, encourages divergent thinking, challenges its members to come up with many possible answers, many ways to handle a situation.

"*C'est une système débrouillarde*," explains Bernice Picard. "*Se débrouiller* means to be able to do anything in any circumstances with whatever you have. Girl Guides helped me a lot because we had to be inventive, even in small things."

59

During the Depression inventiveness was put to practical use. Wright, leader of the First Alberni Guide Company (originally called Princess Mary Guides), wrote in the Guides' *Provincial History of British Columbia:* ''We had very little money to buy uniforms, or anything else, so that many of the Guides and Brownies and most of the Guiders had no uniforms. . . . We assembled what materials we could, dyed them navy blue and brown and made uniforms of a kind . . . for those Guides and Brownies who were without. Somehow we managed to scrounge hats and belts. We made our own ties, socks posed a problem . . . we had to settle for white ones.''

It wasn't that the uniform was important as a regimental item; girls seemed to want to wear it because it identified them with the movement and gave them a greater sense of belonging to the sisterhood. In those early years there must have been hundreds of versions of the Guide uniform as creative leaders and girls across Canada coped with the Depression.

Communication, co-operation, and mutual trust foster an atmosphere which encourages each member to contribute her best. (Right) Brownie Pow-Pow.

In a Guide meeting, it is through the Patrol System that creative (lateral or divergent) thinking is developed on a regular basis. A patrol is a small group of girls: Brownies have sixes; Guides have patrols; Pathfinders have emblem, interest, and social groups; Rangers and Cadets have committees. One of the functions of the patrol is decision-making. To make a decision, one must have considered a number of alternatives. To come up with alternatives, one must brainstorm.

"In a brainstorming session," wrote Dr. Edward De Bono in *Lateral Thinking: A Textbook of Creativity*, "anything goes. No idea is too ridiculous to be put forward. It is important that no attempt at evaluation is made during the brainstorming session. . . . In a brainstorming session one gives out stimulation to others and one receives it from others. Because the different people taking part each tend to follow their own lines of thought, there is less danger of getting stuck with a particular way of looking at the situation."

"Guiding," notes Mary Elizabeth Bayer, "contributes to a group having trust, to members having trust in one another, and to that extent encourages honest searching, honest questions, and hopefully, honest answers. So the brainstorming process is, I think, improved immensely by the Guiding experience. Apart from that it's a lot of fun, and having fun allows one to be more free and imaginative."

Brainstorming is the first step of ISPPE which, as the *Guider Handbook* states, "is the acronym for Investigate, Select, Plan, Participate, and Evaluate" and "was coined for the Canadian Ranger programme. It has come to be used in other branches of Guiding in Canada, because it expresses the kind of programme planning that works best. It is based on the theory that a person is much more likely to be committed to participation in a programme she has helped plan, than to one imposed on her by others."

"Our Guiding should never be a laboured thing," wrote Nadine Corbett in the *Canadian Guider* in 1941. "It will be if we do not realize that we must stick very close to our own Guides, trying all the time to learn their needs and their desires, which vary tremendously from company to company."

"If coming generations can be taught to look on life as a game to be played unselfishly, sportingly, and with a wide vision of all sides of the question," wrote Aline Williams of Madras, India, "then the world will become increasingly better as time goes on."

4

Adventures in Service

"The smile and the good turn are our specialty." —Lord Robert Baden-Powell

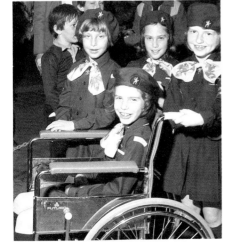

"I promise to help other people every day, especially those at home," says the new Brownie. It's a promise that is enlarged upon with the age and experience of the Guide in a widening world. It's a promise that underlies all the activities undertaken by Guides as they play the great game of Guiding.

"We have most of us met the well-meaning person who is always anxious to help and yet has not the remotest idea what to do, or how to do it. The Guides do not intend to be like that," noted a 1912 news item on the Girl Guide organization.

Through studies in first aid, conservation, outdoor survival techniques, community services, citizenship, and a gamut of other useful subjects, the Guide becomes a resourceful person with a ready store of knowledge to benefit those with whom she comes into contact. She is *prepared* to help both herself and others. Of the four signposts of Guiding — character, skills, fitness, and service — the last is possibly the most important. "Good health, skilled hands, wise head, and kind heart" — it's the kind heart that involves itself in the needs of others.

It is the aim of Guiding to provide opportunities designed to help girls become responsible, resourceful, and happy members of society. The greatest happiness comes from making others happy and that was the spirit in which Guiding was born. It was the practical philosophy of Baden-Powell: "Love," he said in a 1938 speech, "seems to be the prevailing spirit, from the smallest wolf cub up to the Commissioners, and in it lies the secret of our success."

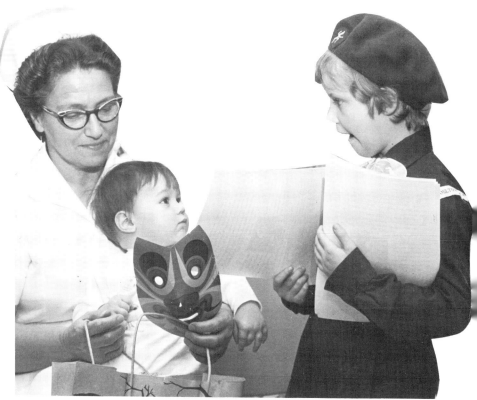

(Top) Brownie with a young hospital patient, *circa* 1969. (Bottom) Gifts are shared. Members of a Brownie Pack and firemen join hands to ensure a bright Christmas for some city children. Brownies are shown with the used toys they collected which, in turn, will be made like new by the firemen for distribution to needy children.

Through the programme, the girl achieves personal satisfaction from learning skills and developing values that make her proud of herself, and of what she can accomplish. At the same time, she learns the importance of working in a community to achieve benefits for the group as a whole—her patrol, unit, home, community at large, country, and finally, her world. She learns how to be of service to herself and to the human family of which she is a part.

This goal of service starts with the Brownie intent on washing dishes or mowing the lawn to help out at home, moves on through the Guide who offers to shop regularly for an immobilized senior citizen and the Pathfinder Guide who assists in the swimming programme for disabled children at a local Y, on to the Ranger unit that aids in the physiotherapy given to a brain-damaged child every Saturday for two years; and on again to the Guiders, Commissioners, Trainers, and others who continue to serve the Girl Guide organization in many volunteer capacities year after year.

A corporation that directs the leisure-time activities of over 274,000 girls across Canada, and is responsible for training and providing current information to 47,000 adult leaders nationwide, must have a professional administrative staff, but that staff is never permitted to undermine the volunteer service foundations of the organization. Girl Guides of Canada–Guides du Canada is founded on the principle that Guiding must never become big business, if it means cutting the organization's roots as a volunteer organization.

The Honourable Betty Clay, daughter of the late Lord and Lady Baden-Powell, expressed this hope at the 1983 Annual Meeting of the Girl Guides of Canada–Guides du Canada: "You must try to ensure that all the Guide Associations with whom you come into contact, and whom the World Association directs, stick to the formula that every Association in the movement must be voluntary, exciting, educational, non-political — a self-motivated training scheme for service open to any girl of any race, nationality, or faith, who is willing to rule her life by our Promise and Law."

"All their lives," wrote Chief Commissioner Nadine Corbett in 1941, "your Guides will know the value of standing shoulder to shoulder with other people for the greater good of all, if you teach them the joy and adventure there is in doing so."

Guiding involves voluntary service at many different levels. There are the women who give their time as Guiders and those who go on to other volunteer positions within the organization, as Commissioners or as Trainers. Still others join the many local associations of the Girl Guides of Canada–Guides du Canada, or offer their services as resource persons. There are innumerable service projects initiated by Guide

units across the country on a continuing basis. Through the Guiding programme the girls give service in their own communities and to world projects as well.

The value system that Guiding instils in its members is not something that easily fades away; it continues to direct girls' lives even after they leave Guiding. In a good many cases, it influences a girl's career choice as she prepares to enter college or the workforce. Among Guiding graduates are policewomen, doctors, politicians, lawyers, ministers, social workers, nurses, and career volunteers — women who have chosen to dedicate their lives to the service of others.

The woman who chooses to progress through the Guiding organization as a volunteer begins her career at either the local-association level or in the role of Guider. Her involvement, like that of her girls, can take her from home to community, to province, to nation, and possibly to the World Association of Girl Guides and Girl Scouts (WAGGGS).

British Columbia Guides planting azaleas in church garden, 1960.

The National Council is the policy-making body of the organization. It studies the trends and interests of Canadian youth and carries out to the best of its ability its function as stated in the Act of Incorporation. Local associations usually meet in a private home or sometimes in the place the girls use for their meetings. They come together as often as is necessary to discuss, plan, and listen. After the necessary business has been conducted, there is often a planned programme— a speaker from within the organization who will broaden members' knowledge of the programme, or perhaps a slide show by a girl who has travelled to an international event, or a camp-fire conducted by one of the units.

Among the fund-raising events that have been successfully organized by local associations in Canada are coffee parties, film shows, thrift shops, toy-repair shops, tours of local-interest sites, progressive dinners, fashion shows, and auctions.

"Every year we'd have a hope chest filled with all the things a bride would need," recalls Val Brown of Newfoundland. "Everyone donated things, made by hand—and when it was full, it would be auctioned off.

Girl Guide cookies are a familiar annual treat for consumers across Canada, and one very tangible way in which the Canadian public shows its support of Guiding.

"We had Cookie Day long before we had an official Cookie Day or commercial cookies. We'd go down in the old hut the night before, and I could see miles and miles of boxes—every Guide had been bothering her mother for weeks before to save the boxes to put the Girl Guide cookies in. And we'd get yards and yards of cellophane, and the Guiders would spend hours preparing these cookies for sale the next day. We'd sell them for 50¢ a box, door to door. It was always a very successful venture. The cookies were always gorgeous!

"I don't think the Guides could possibly have survived without the local associations. In the early days they were there at every call. They were there to do work for us, to help us work, and to make money for us, and I think through the years they've done the same thing."

As the local associations worked to serve their Guide units, so the Guides and Guiders worked to serve their communities.

Baden-Powell wrote in 1914: "The discipline, the health training, the trustworthiness, the skill of different handicrafts, the cheery activity in doing good which the Guide learns, all contribute to make her just the woman who is valuable to her country and to her kind; for, after all, the only true way to win recognition is by deeds, not words—that is, by worthy action, and not by wordy faction."

"I learned a good deal about service through Guides," recalls Barbara Crocker, Executive Assistant to the National Director of Youth Services of the Girl Guides of Canada–Guides du Canada. "Some of what I learned was rather difficult for me to handle.

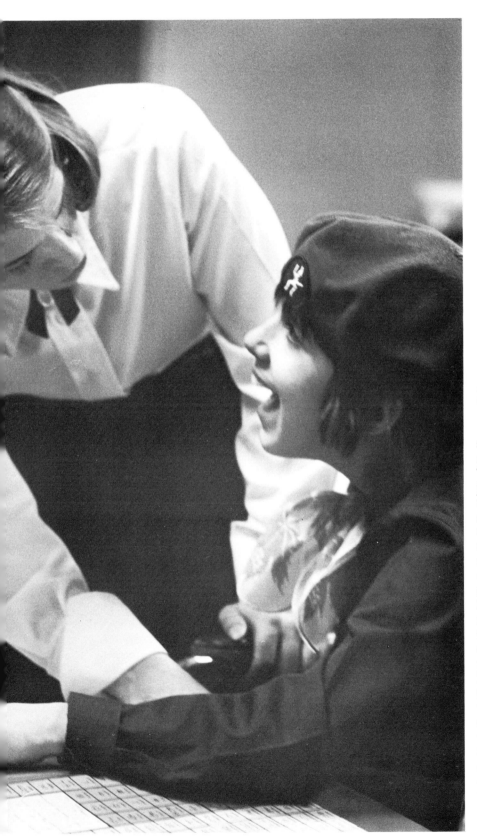

A member of Bloorview Children's Hospital Brownie Pack, 1978.

"When I was a Ranger, we went out and helped at a sanatorium for severely retarded children in Brantford, Ontario. To be exposed to such misfortune was just incredible. I got a lot of help from the girl who went with me on the same night. She seemed to handle it so well, and I thought to myself, 'What's wrong with me that she can cope and she actually looks forward to going, when I think about it all day in school and think, what am I going to do?' I have to remember not to jump when they wheel that kid into the room and things like that. Yet, she was very cool about it, and smiled and so forth, so I took my cue from her, really, and I learned a lot from her. And yet she was not one of the more outgoing kids in the Ranger group. She was quieter, determined, always seeming to go along with what the group had planned rather than joining in on the planning. She was a very stable influence on our group of six to eight girls—all of whom had come up together through Guides. This girl eventually became a nurse."

Guide service projects often centre around disabled young people and senior citizens. The December 1970 issue of the Guide magazine *Alive* carried an article on a Midland, Ontario, Ranger group that won an important international Guiding award for working hard for several years to help a crippled youngster learn to move properly. The award was the W.D. Ross Perpetual Trophy, "awarded every year to the group in Guiding—anywhere in the world—making the most outstanding contribution to the community."

"The [Midland] girls started helping little Penny Kitchen in 1966 when she was four years old and unable to crawl, sit up, or even turn over. She could not feed herself or talk. . . . Penny's parents had taken her to the Institute for the Achievement of Human Potential in Philadelphia, where radical treatment was undertaken for brain-damaged youngsters. . . . The doctors at the clinic said that not all the brain cells were damaged, therefore the undamaged ones had to be taught to do the work of the others. This is done through a series of exercises called 'patterning movements.'

"At least three people were needed to put Penny through patterning movements—one at the head and one at each side for her arms and legs. They moved Penny in a certain pattern prescribed by the doctors. The exercises were repeated six times a day. . . . The Rangers took over treatments every Saturday morning. Not only did they carry out the patterning, but they played with Penny, helped with dishes, ran errands, and became Penny's favourite friends."

The 1965 winner of the Ross Trophy was a group of Girls Scouts from the Philippines who rallied to help the

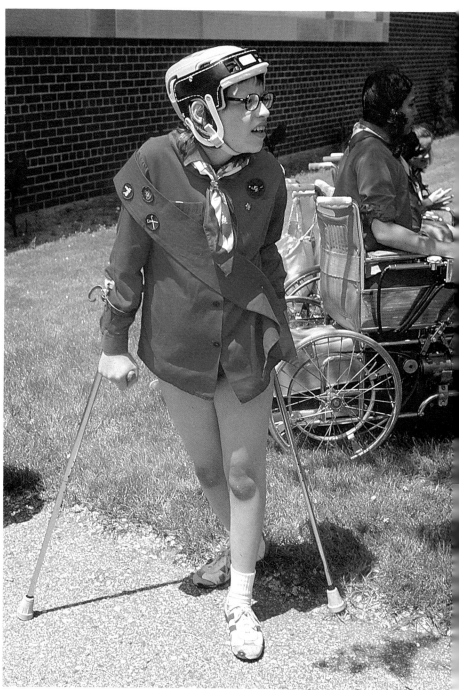

people in an area stricken by a volcanic eruption. The Girl Scouts set up a centre for children on the grounds of an elementary school. An article in the April 1967 issue of *Alive* described the project: "Working under adult supervision, Girl Scouts came to help put up tents, set up washing areas, and make gadgets for tables and other needs. They helped round up refugee children and urged them to come every day to the centre for food, baths, games, and lessons. . . . This wonderful service project went on for two months. A total of 900 Girl Scouts worked at the centre, looking after nearly 2,000 children. Altogether the girls gave 20,000 hours of their time."

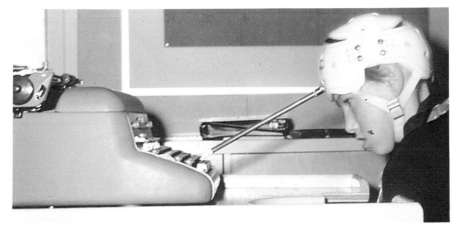

Guiders too may become involved in work with disadvantaged, destitute, or disabled children. The Extension Department of the Girl Guides, first started as an experiment in a hospital in England, was established in Canada in 1930, and brought Guiding to invalids and girls in hospitals. Guiding for the disabled had its own challenges, as provincial histories record. "Getting patients in and out of uniforms is always a problem," noted an Alberta report. "Yet the uniform is such an important part of Guiding to them that it is worth the effort and ingenuity. In the Calgary Hospital Company most of the uniforms are split down the back and tied, with sleeves open at the seams."

(Below) Three members of a Girl Guide Company with their Gold Cords, 1964. (Right) Brownies at Belleville School for the Deaf.

"As Guiders," wrote one of the leaders of the First Tranquille Company, in 1962, in a hospital for mentally retarded girls in British Columbia, "we learned to be very adaptable and quick to read the mood of the company. Although we always planned the meetings, we certainly could not always use the programme we had intended . . . and more often than not we had to change either part or all of it at the drop of a hat. Once we had to give it up completely and I took them all home with me for coffee."

"As one of the most important functions of the Guide programme for girls with disabilities is to make them feel part of the community group, many outings are planned with regular companies, and these are most successful. Deaf Guides have assisted at blood-donor clinics and coffee parties and formed the colour party for the first Gold Cord Presentation Ceremony at the Legislative Building in 1965," wrote Barbara Villy Cormack in *Landmarks*, a history of Guiding in Alberta. She pointed out that several of the former Guides from the Alberta School for the Deaf went on to the Gallaudet College for the Deaf in Washington, D.C., and graduated as teachers, librarians, and lab technicians.

The organization's policy is to integrate Guides with disabilities as much as possible with active companies and packs, thereby lessening the sense of difference. Many packs and companies across the country today have disabled girls as regular members. Each girl, whether she is disabled or not, works at her own speed; this is the key to successful integration, which is demonstrated time and again today.

One of the most exciting, most successful, and undoubtedly most enjoyable Guiding experiences for disabled girls is the annual Explorations Camp organized by the Ontario Council. At this camp Guides with disabilities and those without enjoy and learn from one another. It is one of the highlights of the Ontario Guiding year.

Helping out in wartime has been another important service function performed by Guides. Although the early Guides were somewhat put off by Agnes Baden-Powell's insistence on bandaging, first aid, and aid to the wounded in battle, her call for girls to be prepared to help in time of war was very relevant by 1914.

"In this time of National Crisis and grave danger," exhorted the *Girl Guides' Gazette* (London, England) during the First World War, "the Girl Guides also can give valuable help to the country by carrying out the duties for which they have been trained and organized. The Headquarters' Committee appeal to the patriotism of Girl Guides to give voluntary assistance in every way in their power.

"To help locally by offering service locally to Red Cross Detachments, St. John's Ambulance or the nearest Hospital Organization; offering service locally to relief committees, when organized, and to serve in soup kitchens, creches, etc.; offering services to Soldiers and Sailors Help Society. Their needs are for Convalescent Homes, cyclists for messages, laundry, cookery, and home nursing; by undertaking cooking, needlework, and laundry work for hospitals if required; by giving household assistance to families in distress or in case of illness; by offering to take charge of children while their mothers are out at work."

The First World War may not have directly affected Canadian Guides, but they too would be called into service in 1940. All across Canada Brownies, Guides, Rangers, and Leaders were knitting, salvaging, bundling, bandaging, and working in hundreds of innovative ways to aid the war effort.

"In Halifax," wrote Nancy Bowden Hutchins, in *Guides, All Guides*, "where

Older Guides help at the Red Cross Lodge, Shaughnesy Military Hospital, *circa* 1940.

warships docked or rode at anchor, where passenger and cargo ships awaited convoy, where contingents of army, navy, and airforce embarked for duty abroad, Girl Guides and their leaders were constantly close to and aware of the war and its demands upon civilians. Guides throughout the Halifax–Dartmouth area aided the Women's Volunteer Service, which had set up a Medicine Bottle Exchange at its headquarters to overcome a shortage of bottles in sick bays and hospitals."

"All St. John's was war effort," remembers former outport nurse Jane Hutchings. "We were blacked out, we were a big base, and we were rationed. It was nothing to see the men coming in from a big ship that had been torpedoed. Your moms were knitting, and people you knew were making cakes for the Caribou Hut, a place put up by the German War Veterans' Association. It was turned into a place for soldiers and sailors and army people to meet. There was someone there to mend their clothes, and they had a writing room. And there was a canteen going from early morning to nine o'clock at night. It was manned by volunteers from all over Newfoundland. Guides went down sometimes to entertain, and then, when we were old enough, we joined staff, and we were allowed to go down and work on Saturdays."

Anne du Moulin's first job as a social worker was to set up a centre for the children of the war workers at East Kitsilano, British Columbia. At the time, Anne was Public Relations Commissioner for the Greater Vancouver Girl Guides.

"They came from all over Canada to build ships, to make money, and to help with the war effort, presumably. So usually mum and dad were working, and the children were in a totally strange environment. Nobody, really, to supervise them or to keep them out of trouble. . . . My job was to try and set up a centre that could alleviate this problem and prevent kids from getting into all kinds of trouble. . . . We were able to recruit a lot of help to organize games and programmes for these kids from senior Guides around the area. Seniors were about fifteen or sixteen years old then, so they were a great help as leaders for the younger kids."

Anne started her Guiding in Kingston, Ontario, in 1932, but it was really at Queen Margaret School in Duncan, British Columbia, that she caught the Guiding bug. There she went through the levels, along with many other girls, of Guide, Lieutenant Captain, and so on. As a young adult she went on to become Provincial Public Relations Secretary of Manitoba, and she's been Training Commissioner for Manitoba. She was elected to the National Council in the 1970s. Now semi-retired, she continues to offer her services as a resource person for trainings.

"The value system represented in the Promise and the Law," she says, "are irrevocably directing my life, whether or not I happen to wear a pin or a hat or what-have-you."

And she has many to wear, should she wish to. Decorated in 1967 for

service to national orgranizations during her presidency of the Canadian Organization of Social Workers, she is the proud owner of the Centennial Medal of Canada and of the Guiding Beaver, "granted to members for outstanding service to the Girl Guides of Canada–Guides du Canada." Her own professional association awarded her its prestigious McArton Award for service to the community through the profession of social work.

From her early girlhood in Guiding, service has been second nature to Anne.

"You're given a life-long warrant when you're enrolled," she says as she recounts the story of her career choice. "When I was in about third-year university—I was taking a B.A., you know, where you never make up your mind—well, about the third year, I heard something about the fact that

they were starting a new thing at the School of Social Work on campus called 'group work,' which taught you how to help people in groups. And so I thought to myself, 'Well, this sounds familiar!' I'd already been a Guide Lieutenant and Captain for a few years by this time. Suddenly the light dawned and I thought, 'You know, I could get paid for doing something that I've enjoyed and loved doing as a volunteer all these years. Wouldn't that be something? And I could be on my own, and I wouldn't have to live at the family home and be a burden to them. It should have been more noble than that; but really, I found out I could get a salary for doing what I'd been doing and loving for the past twelve or so years. The light had suddenly turned on, and I made the connection, and there was no question that that's what I wanted to do.''

Service projects are an integral part of Guiding: from tagging children at the Canadian National Exhibition (top left) and providing first aid in emergency situations to the local clean-up, Guides are among the first to volunteer their services.

One of the most remarkable contributions of the adult members of the Girl Guide organization to the war effort was the formation of the Guide International Service (GIS). This was a voluntary adult program set up in 1944 to provide help in the rehabilitation of those countries that had suffered during the war. The first training camp for the GIS was held at Queen Margaret School in Duncan, British Columbia. Two trainees from this camp were selected to represent Canada on GIS teams overseas. They were Guiders Hortense Warne (to Germany) and Betty Jane Fleming (to service as a registered nurse in Hanover); both were from British Columbia.

When the war was over, Guides and Guiders returned to local peacetime service and to personal citations of bravery. Mrs. Phyllis Munday recounts the act that won her a Bronze Cross, the highest award for valour granted by the Girl Guide organization: "We were living in a cabin up on Grouse Mountain; in those days there was nothing but a trail to walk up, about 3,500 feet above Vancouver, and there were very few people on the mountain.

One day when there was snow on the ground, two youths came up. These boys persisted in sliding right in front of our cabin on the very edge of the bluff, which was all trees then. One of them dashed in and told us that the other one had gone over the cliffs. So I went down in among the trees. It was much too slippery—we didn't have mountain boots like they have now. I found him. I thought he'd been killed, but I found he was breathing.

"Then my husband came down also. Between us we got a rope. I had to get it onto the lad and drag him out to the trees so that I could use the trees to save him from slipping farther. Eventually I got him onto a toboggan. My job then was to hold the toboggan from above because we were going along a very steep sidehill—the tail of the toboggan would slide down unless we could hook up to a tree.

(Above) At Queen Margaret's School, Duncan, B.C., Guides sorted and packed paper salvage for the war effort, *circa* 1942. (Right) No camping programme is complete without a drill in life-saving skills. Pilot Camp, Doe Lake, Ontario, 1957. (Far right) Guider Phyllis Munday was awarded the Bronze Cross for saving the life of a young mountain tobogganer.

"It took about three hours to get him up. When we got him in, I was sure he'd be dead, but I could feel a pulse. I had a St. John's Ambulance Certificate, so when I got him into the cabin, I knew I shouldn't move him; and I knew from training that when a person is thoroughly chilled he shouldn't be heated suddenly, so I wrapped him in a blanket. I collected hot water in my two hot-water bottles and a number of jam jars, and I placed those round him.

"By the time the doctor got up the hill, the boy had begun to breathe better. His head had been injured too. We found he had a concussion. The doctor said if we hadn't got him up so quickly, he wouldn't have lived. I nursed him for six weeks before he could be moved. His sister eventually became one of my Guides."

"Guiding taught me about people," says Her Honour Donna J. Haley, a County Court judge in Toronto, Ontario, "particularly in camp situations, because I was an only child. And when I went to camp I found all these people and they all fit into a slot, and you had to work with them, and so on, and you got some of the corners knocked off. I began to appreciate people much differently than I had before. I think that experience was a very great contribution to me as a person.

"In Guiding, you learn over the years to understand the other fellow's point of view, and you acquire a certain compassion. The Promise and the Law really did affect my outlook and my approach to the challenges I have met as a lawyer."

People skills are what RCMP Constable Cheryl La Fosse of Newfoundland acquired through Guiding. Cheryl was the first woman to be enrolled in the RCMP College, in 1974. In 1981 she joined a Guide camp in a different role —that of security officer on night patrol! It was a moving experience, she confessed, that brought back fond memories of her own early days at Guide camp.

One wouldn't immediately think of library science as a service-oriented career, and yet this is how Sheila Laidlaw sees her work as head Librarian at the University of New Brunswick.

"There is today a bibliographic instruction trend in libraries," says Sheila, "from custodianship to service, and my Guiding background in terms of service and helping people fits right into this trend. The skills I acquire in library workshops I will interchange with skills I use in Guiding. Networking—the sharing of expertise from one field to another, from one part of the country to another—certainly goes on. The involvement of Guiding people in other volunteer organizations is another side to this networking. For example, a number of us were at the founding meeting of the new New Brunswick Association of Adult Education recently. The Guide organization is providing leadership education in

countless communities across the country that have adult-education programmes. The formal setting is the community college, but the informal network includes organizations such as Guiding, and those of us who have had training in adult leadership.

"So who's the Professor and who's the Volunteer? More and more the 'outside' world is acknowledging that Guiding has a role to play with the adults in the community as well as with the youngsters. I know that some people have taught in community colleges across Canada, not because of their educational background, but because of their Guide experience and training."

Guiding was "always part of school" for Jane Hutchings. At Bishop Spenser College, all the units met on Mondays.

One just automatically joined Brownies and went on to Guides. All the schools had Guide companies in the 1930s. "The Model school had a Guide Company, the Salvation Army school, the United Church school. Our uniforms were all navy blue with white collars and cuffs for Spenser, and different ties. And we had our badges right on the sleeves of our school uniforms.

"Everything I learned that was extracurricular," says Jane, "—darning, cooking, sewing—was from Guiding. Then, when it came to first aid and home nursing, we went to the General Hospital and we were taught right there to make beds and the rest. We were right in there with the nurses, and I think all of us became interested in nursing because of that.

At camp a girl learns to appreciate the roles of harmony and mutual dependency in nature and in life.

"About 1933-34, little Lucy Harris was lost on the south coast of New-foundland. She was found after ten days and brought into St. John's. They had to amputate both her legs. And I remember we were so excited in Guides because we raised enough money to buy her a bedjacket, and Miss Manuel took us all down to the ward, and we were allowed to stand outside the door as she took in the present and gave it to her. So you sort of grew up knowing that hospitals were places where people were helped. That was my first experience with nursing. Then I did my first aid there, and finally studied nursing there.

"Guiding was a big part of our life at Bishop Spenser School. You were always doing something for people, so I suppose in a way it made a difference to me in wanting to be a nurse."

All members of Guiding have fond memories of camp!

"The service ideal permeated all the activities at the First Huntsville [Ontario] Guide Company," recalls Andrea Alexander. "It is absolutely reflected in what I have done with my life in the last fifteen years."

Andrea is currently Past-President of the Toronto Symphony Women's Committee and is a Representative for the TSO on the International Association of Major Symphony Orchestra Volunteer Committees.

"It is the Junior Women's Committee with which I started. It does all the educational programmes for the symphony—concerts for children, special events for young people, anything that goes into the schools. This committee is made up of about thirty-five adult members at any one time, so it's a very big workload for each person. Then, once you move along through vice-president, president, and past-president, it's three or four years of 100 per cent business. Early on you get singled out because you do something in a reasonable way—and you get into it like a full-time job, except it's in the volunteer sector."

Guiding was a very strong influence in Andrea's life in the small town of Huntsville.

"I went in as a Guide. I joined because it was the thing to do in this small town to be with your friends. It was exciting. They provided interesting things to do—I have wonderful memories of mid-week camp suppers in a local park—and fine leadership."

Andrea's own leadership potential was developed by a combination of Guiding and family role models. Her mother was "the first woman elected to the Huntsville Board of Education and the first woman appointed to the Session of the United Church." An aunt rose to become Division Commissioner in Guides. Andrea herself quickly became a patrol leader in her unit, and earned her Gold Cord.

"Had I wanted to become a biochemist or a physicist, my parents wouldn't have thought it unusual," says Andrea, reflecting upon her career choice. "It was just very natural for me to have chosen teaching."

It was a happy choice, for her experience with various Boards of Education has proven an invaluable asset in her work as a volunteer for the Toronto Symphony and other arts organizations.

If Guiding develops in the girl a genuine desire to do service for others, it gives her in return camaraderie, skills, and recognition for achievement, as well as a number of other tangible rewards. You "learn more about yourself, have fun and interesting experiences, learn new skills and gain confidence, test out areas of interest and gain experience in future careers, [and] meet a variety of people of different backgrounds, ages and interests," according to a Guide Volunteer Centre brochure calling for student involvement.

Marshmallows always taste good on your fingertips!

Brown Owl tells a story, *circa* **1968.**

For Elizabeth Hann, former Mayor of Corner Brook, Newfoundland, Guiding proved a pathway to a fuller spiritual life.

"My involvement in Guiding started quite accidentally. We had some Guiding units in our Salvation Army church, and as a member of the Group Committee and the Fund-Raising Committee for the church, I was approached by one of our Brownie Leaders on one occasion in 1977, when she was unable to get to the Brownie camp due to illness in the family. Not wanting to disappoint the little girls in getting to their camp, I took on the responsibility of attending the camp with them, and they just stole my heart—lock, stock, and barrel. And I've been with the unit ever since as Brown Owl.

"I wasn't as involved with my church as I should have been in 1977. Working with the children brought me much closer to the church, because you can't teach a child unless they can see by your example that you *are* what you are trying to teach them to be. I think that being in the forefront with the children, trying to teach them that they should uphold their Promise and Law and do their duty to their God and country, made me realize that I needed a closer affiliation with my church."

These have been but a few examples of how Guiding benefits not only the society it serves, but also the individual it involves. On a larger scale, Guiding in peacetime, as it did in two world wars, continues to apply its conscience to the sufferings of mankind.

5

Adventures in Friendship

"A Guide is
a friend to all,
and a sister to
every Guide."
—The Guide Law

The World Association of Girl Guides and Girl Scouts (WAGGGS), of which the Girl Guides of Canada–Guides du Canada is a Charter Member, was formed in 1928 to link together the many national organizations of Girl Guides and Girl Scouts. Its object, as stated in its constitution, is "through co-operation to promote unity of purpose and common understanding in the fundamental principles of Girl Guiding and Girl Scouting throughout the world, and to encourage friendship among all girls of all nations, within frontiers and beyond."

It was in this spirit of friendship, co-operation, and appreciation of a common bond that, in 1962, membership within the Girl Guides of Canada–Guides du Canada was extended to the Guides Catholiques du Canada (*secteur français*). Guides Catholiques du Canada (*secteur français*) is affiliated with the Girl Guides of Canada–Guides du Canada by a special agreement that grants them the right to autonomy in matters of programme, training, appointment of officers, and finance. They must conform to the principles of Guiding as laid down by the Founder and to the policies of the Girl Guides of Canada–Guides du Canada. Their programme, training, and literature are designed to suit the particular needs of French-speaking Roman Catholic girls. They print their own publications in the French language and have their own uniforms. The *Guides Catholiques* has three age groups: Jeanettes (nine to eleven years); Guides (twelve to fourteen years); and Kamsok (fifteen to seventeen years).

Guides Catholiques recognize the Chief Commissioner of the Girl Guides of Canada–Guides du Canada as the head of Guiding in Canada. They have representation on the National Council, and their membership is included in the national figures. However, any French-speaking Roman Catholic girl who wishes to become a member of the Girl Guides of Canada–Guides du Canada may do so.

The World Association of Girl Guides and Girl Scouts, with Headquarters in London, England, and with a current membership of 104 countries, meets triennially to assess the past and plan for the future of Guiding around the world. WAGGGS has four world centres —Sangam (Poona, India), Our Chalet (Adelboden, Switzerland), Our Cabaña (Cuernavaca, Mexico), and Olave House (London England). "By means of correspondence and interchange of visits," wrote Baden-Powell, "we are helping to build the foundation for the eventual establishment of common interests and friendships, which will ultimately and automatically bring about disarmament and world peace."

Sir Robert may have been somewhat idealistic about disarmament and world peace, but there is no doubt that Guiding and Scouting, through the concept of international sisterhood and brotherhood, combat the kind of bigotry that can lead to discord in a community, and ultimately to war in our world. Each time a Guide is enrolled, the ceremony ends with the words, "You are now one of the sisterhood of Guides."

"The Girl Guides," wrote Baden-Powell in 1918, "are a sisterhood. This means that members of it, from top to bottom, are working together as sisters...from joy of the work. It is not a small army composed of officers, non-commissioned officers and privates in their respective grades, directed or directing under imposed instruction."

Members of the organization talk of the "Guiding family," and certainly this sense of belonging is shared by many girls and women on a variety of levels. For the only child, Guiding becomes a chance to experience sisterhood; for a girl from a large family, Guiding perhaps provides an opportunity to be noticed as an individual and to be exposed to activities for which her own large family has little time; for many girls the Guider may be a confidante, a third party to whom she can express her troubles and concerns; to the sheltered girl, who, for whatever reasons, has been unable to realize her own potential, Guiding can provide a support group that builds self-confidence.

For young women past Ranger age, there is LINK for women eighteen to thirty. It allows them to come together and share memories of their Guiding sisterhood and to create new ones. For those who have temporarily left Guiding, the family can be found again when needed; a Guide in a new town need never be lonely. For older women who wish to share Guiding memories and cherish that sisterhood, there is the Trefoil Guild. For girls and Guiders transferred overseas, there are Companies and Packs on Foreign Soil. For members visiting India, Switzerland, England, and Mexico, there are the world centres waiting to welcome them and put them in touch with sisters in those countries.

Like any happy family, the Guiding family knows how to have a good time. It takes every opportunity to get members together for fun. Rallies, camps, international trips, seminars, conferences, and other such activities bring girls and leaders together to share good times, good ideas, and much laughter. There are also occasions for Guides to get together with Boy Scouts for joint activities such as service projects, camps, dances, and ski meets. But it is the nurturing environment of the sisterhood that keeps girls in Guiding; the fact that it provides an environment in which a girl can become her best possible self, where she can make mistakes and not be put down, where her special psychological, physiological, and intellectual potential to make a contribution to society and to the betterment of her species will be understood and developed.

Current studies indicate that this function operates in most women's organizations in this country. A brother is fun to have sometimes, but he can certainly inhibit you in a good many situations. There are things that you just can't talk to him about. He just isn't the same as a sister. Although some countries do have joint Guide/Scout organizations, many others have found that the all-female organization allows girls a good deal more freedom than the co-ed one.

As Linda Hoffman, a member of one of the committed nuclear families within the extended family of Guiding, puts it: "As an all-female organization, guiding has its own special identity, and I think girls need that. They need to associate with something they know is their own. When girls get together with boys, they act entirely differently —and when they're with girls, I find they're more themselves. They can let their hair down and be what they are! I feel we're liberated."

"Guiding seems to have an effect even where it's not immediately ob-

vious," says Barbara Crocker. Guiding gives a girl something lasting. She may not always be able to identify it immediately, but it will invariably surface at some point in her life. Often the girl who just enjoys coming to Guides and is not interested in earning an armful of badges will recognize what she has gained and return as a leader. Almost inevitably the sisterhood of Guiding leads to enduring friendships outside the context of the organization.

"Outside Guiding all my girls used to call me Aunt Edith," recalls Edith Temple, a former Division Commissioner at Ste. Anne-de-Bellevue, Quebec. "I used to have informal get-togethers with them at my house on Sunday mornings after church. Well, one day we were having a discussion about religion, and God, the Guide Law, and the Religion in Life Badge. And one of the girls said: 'Aunt Edith, I don't believe in God.' It threw me for a minute and then I said, 'Oh . . . you don't?' I didn't speak to her right then, but later asked her to stay for a short while.

You're never too old for Guiding fun! Now there's LINK, for women age 18 to 30 who are temporarily inactive in Guiding but who, nevertheless, want to keep in touch with the organization.

Christian Religion and Life badge.

Jewish Religion and Life badge.

"The others had all left, and I sat down and asked her why. She said, 'Oh, I don't know, I just don't think there's any such thing as God.' She couldn't really explain herself very well; she was about thirteen, I imagine. I said, 'Well, there are so many reasons that make me know there is a God.' She said, 'Like what?' So I explained: 'Like the beauty of the earth, children, having a child, and things like that.' And she kind of cried a little bit, and said, 'You're going to be disappointed in me?' And I said, 'Oh, no, I'd never be disappointed in you. I just want you to think about it sometimes.'

"She remained in Guides for a while, and then she went to college. One year I received a little note from her: 'Dear Aunt Edith, everything's fine with me. . . . You might be glad to know that I'm President of the Religious Association at College.'

"To me, that was one of the experiences that made Guiding very worth while."

"I remember the really good feelings," says Pat Lepper. "I remember

my Brownie leader; she's still a friend of my mother's. I dropped out of Guiding when I was in high school. I only got back into Guiding about two years ago. I had come up to Sault Ste. Marie to work as a metallurgical engineer. I didn't know very many people, and on one of the many tours in the plant, I ran into a woman who recognized my name through my mother, and said, 'Oh, you're very involved in Guiding.' 'No, I'm not; I haven't been for about ten years now,' I said. We spoke for a while, and I realized that I had subconsciously wanted to get involved in something up here that would help me to meet people and help me to do some good. That's how I got back into Guiding. I've been a Brown Owl for two years now. I've been to a few trainings, and I'm really, really enjoying it."

"The feeling was camaraderie, really," reflects Dorothy McBride, Secretary Treasurer of Doubleday Canada Ltd., an ardent Guider and currently Music Adviser for the Highland Glen Division in Ontario. "It was doing things

with other people, being part of a group and really pulling together that I enjoyed. I came from a large family so that was all quite normal for me, knowing that everybody works together and all that. I guess it was just an extension of my own family. I just felt we were all one great big family, but they were all new friends, and there were all these new and exciting things to do. Guiding gave me opportunities to do a lot of things I would never had had the opportunity to do because of my economic background.

"My Guide Captain used to take me on bird hikes, for example. She taught me, and right now I'm very keen on birding. She used to take me on Sunday mornings. We'd go to church at eight o'clock, and then we'd go off and have a breakfast hike, and she'd take her binoculars along, and we'd take turns using them. She introduced me to birding, and it's still part of my life.

"She also took me to the art gallery, and that was foreign to my family. When I was a Cadet, the group of girls I was a Cadet with had all been brought up on classical music. They introduced me to it, and it's one of my great loves today. Guiding has been really good to me."

93

A group of young Guiders at Banff School of Fine Arts pose with their resource leader. Representatives in this group are from India, Germany, Mexico, U.S.A., Great Britain, and Canada.

Barbara Brush is Assistant to the Director of Programming for the Anglican Diocese in Ottawa. "Programming," she says, "includes everything that happens in the church—missions, outreach, Christian education, and so forth. I help the people in the Diocese of Ottawa to understand what their ministry is, help the Diocese produce the newsletter that goes out to members once a month, help to make television programmes, and help with the running of the Christian education programme."

Barbara attributes much of her success as a professional to the training she received through Guiding: "When I was eleven, I had my appendix out, and my heart stopped on the operating table. Because of that, I was protected within my home environment. In Guiding, I was given the opportunity to try things out all the time, and I was continuously challenged. Going out and doing things helped me gather back my strength. Through all the positions I later held in Guiding, I've been given the opportunity to grow, learn, and interact with people."

What of the girl who has shared the fun and laughter of the Guiding sisterhood for most of her life, and then, at eighteen, finds she is too old to continue being a Girl Guide? Because she is busy with college or work, she cannot take on the role of leader. Barbara Wolfe, Heather Earnshaw, Phillipa Cureton, Elizabeth Fiander, and Lois Found are all young women in this situation. Through LINK they have found a way to keep in touch with each other and with the organization.

"Ours is a student group, registered at the University of Guelph," says Philippa. "People can find out about us through the regular university channels, so that any girls who have been Guides or Rangers who come to Guelph University can find out about LINK and join us. Being registered with the university also gives us certain privileges on campus—meeting rooms, the right to sell our cookies, and that sort of thing."

"I'm working full time now," says Elizabeth Fiander, "I don't go to school. I started with LINK at the university and I've continued the association now that I'm at work."

Members of LINK set together to share Guiding memories and to participate in a variety of social activities, including ski weekends.

The group has been together four years. None of the girls knew each other before the "link" was made.

"It's really neat because you get together, and you already have the link of Guiding. You share the same interests. One of the most exciting events is our annual ski weekend. The first weekend back at school after the Christmas holidays we all take off and go cross-country skiing and camp out for the weekend. Right now, we're planning a barbecue with the Rovers from the University of Guelph.

"When we did the cookie sale at the college last April, there were a bunch of people who came up to us and said, 'You're still Girl Guides? You're too old to be Girl Guides!' But it's so much fun to get together and laugh and sing, remember different camps. I suppose there's a lot of nostalgia to it, but you're doing new things as well. You've already got a connection, and you're continuing it.

"LINK opens up a whole new area of recruitment for Guide Leaders. Communication is important, and LINK keeps you in touch. So when you're ready to become a Leader, you won't be saying, 'Oh, fifteen years ago when I was a Guide!' You'll know what's gone on currently in the organization. For girls who may join us at college and who have never been in Guides, it gives them good exposure. They learn all about Guiding, and it will prepare them for the time when they might possibly become Leaders. Eventually, probably most of us will become Leaders because we're just enthusiastic enough to pass it on. We want to share that with kids coming up. Right now, we're all too busy to have a unit, but we want to keep up our enthusiasm and share it with others our own age." 95

There's nothing like a good party to bring people together! Guiding sisters from around the world enjoyed this one at the "Guiding on the Move", International Camp, Cape Breton, N.S., 1977.

World Camp, Doe Lake, 1957.

There are LINK members scattered across the country. In fall of 1983 the Ontario members held their first provincial event at National Headquarters in Toronto. The purpose was to pool ideas and plan for future expansion and better communication between isolated members.

For children of Canadians abroad, there are Companies and Packs on Foreign Soil, carried on through the support of the Department of National Defence and External Affairs. The groups are under the supervision of the Commissioner for Companies and Packs on Foreign Soil and her committee. Close contact with Girl Guide/Scout associations in these countries provides many opportunities for international experience.

Stories involving the international aspect of Guiding are many, but perhaps one touching episode recounted in *Sixty Years and More*, a provincial history of Guiding in British Columbia, will serve to illustrate the priceless bond of friendship that Guiding introduces between strangers.

"After World War II, all over the world people were trying to gather up the threads of their old lives, and the newspapers were filled with the stories of those unfortunates who had lost family, home, and country, thousands who were bewildered, and lost. One day in a small town in British Columbia, a letter arrived from a girl in Germany requesting old Scout or Guide uniforms. A Guider replied, and the following quotations from the German girl's reply give some idea of the value of this contact...

" 'You cannot even imagine what it meant to me, that at last I found contact with the outer world. This letter full of help and good wishes was like a bit of sunshine in our grey life.... Yesterday we had again our meeting.... I had to see that everyone has entered her good doings on her card. I do not know whether you have this custom.... The last half hour we spend singing and learning songs.... It is only the difficulty that we have no books. I have only one called *Tenderfoot to King's Scout* but this if for boys. If you can, please do send me one like it for girls. Please do not send more than one because there is nobody except me who can handle it. I shall translate it and make copies for our group.

" 'I must tell you something about where and how and among whom we are living. Please try to imagine a very flat country. As it is everywhere out of town there are villages in a few miles distance. Once there were fields between them, but now these spaces are filled with camps, where during the Nazi time the foreign workers were living, one can also call it imprisoned. Wooden barracks, without wooden floors or ceilings. When it is windy, in the rooms it is windy too. These barracks are filled with Displaced Persons, and with German Refugees, people thrown out of the parts of Germany that belong now to USSR, Poland, etc. All these people have lost everything. Many families have not for every member of their family a bed or a chair.... There are mostly no fathers, because the men have been taken to concentration camps and labour camps before they were allowed to leave their former home.... I have seen very many people and I have seen what it means to belong to the conquerers and the conquered.... I worked for the living of my parents, as my father was badly injured during a bombing—he lost his right arm. Perhaps this is the reason that I now go back to the idea of Scouting, to the Laws which I think I am now understanding better, and to the ideas of friendship between all people. Also from this point of view I thank you once more for your wish to help us, because I am sure that your letter and the parcels will give me an opportunity of showing my girls what I meant about being a friend to every other person and a sister to every other Girl Guide. Please give my special thanks to all your girls and be sure that you are doing a wonderful thing in remaining our friends.'

"So the Guider and her Guides sent off uniforms, and a long term relationship was established.... When the German girl married and had a little daughter, the Canadian Guider became the child's godmother."

Although correspondence between Guides is somewhat more organized today, it is still a very happy part of the international face of Guiding. The International Post Box handles correspondence between Guiders, Guides, Pathfinders, Rangers, Cadets, and Junior Leaders in Canada and those in other countries. Anyone who wishes to have a pen pal in another country may do so by completing the application/postcard available from provincial offices.

Skills to learn, service to render, and friends to share your dreams.

Participants in international events, which bring Guides from all over the world together for special camps and similar activities, are finally selected by National Headquarters. Elizabeth Hill, Printing and Publishing Administrator for the Headquarters, recalls the thrill of a trip to Switzerland for the 1957 Centenary World Camp: "It gave me an opportunity to meet and come to know girls my own age—I was fifteen at the time—from around the world, as well as to enjoy the adventure of travel to three foreign countries. The fifty girls selected to attend the World Camp in Switzerland travelled overseas on the ocean liner *The Empress of Britain* with fifty Canadian girls who were attending a camp in England the same year. Our European itinerary included a few days in London and a trek by train to the Vallée de Conches, Switzerland, where we camped for about two weeks with Swiss Guides. While in Switzerland, we saw The Matterhorn, visited Our Chalet, and attended a rally at which Lady Baden-Powell was present. From Switzerland we went by train to Paris, where we spent three days sightseeing. Prior to returning home to Canada, we stayed at a youth hostel in Chester, England. Then it was back to the ship for the return voyage to Montreal!

"It was a six-week trip all-told, and I can really say that I grew up in that time. When I think back, I realize that one of the greatest advantages of the event was the length of time we girls spent together. This was before the time of air travel, remember. Those days we spent on the ship allowed for the making of many life-long friendships. In fact, we have kept in touch, many of us. Recently about fourteen of us and one leader met in Toronto for a three-day reunion. It was wonderful how the years just fell away as memories were exchanged. Guiding, and the opportunity to travel to the Centenary Camp in Switzerland in 1957 to experience first-hand the sisterhood of Guiding on a global scale, have certainly enriched my life enormously."

Erin Cole, sixteen, of Burnaby, British Columbia, one of the Canadian girls selected for the Stichting Haarlem Jamborette in the Netherlands in 1983, was also moved by this sense of sisterhood.

"At the end of the two-week stay, we were all very sad to be leaving camp because we had made friendships that we hope will last all our lives."

It is through WAGGGS that international exchange takes place. Through the Canadian World Friendship Fund,

Canadian Guides and Guiders contribute to travel into and out of the country so that girls and leaders can share international opportunities.

"Just as we help our own membership with travel costs going out of the country," explains Dr. Marion (Pip) Rogers, member of the WAGGGS Constitutions Committee, "so we assist girls from other member countries coming to Canada to enjoy our events and home hospitality here."

Working situations are another way for Guides and leaders to get together.

"The World Association meets every three years in a different country and at that time Canada sends a delegation," reports Marion. "No matter what the delegation size, each country has only one vote at a World Conference. This insures that the special needs of tiny countries are considered and dealt with as democratically as possible, and that everyone has an equally important voice and opinion.

"Between these triennial meetings, the World Committee, twelve members elected by the delegates to the World Conference, work on the day-to-day matters affecting Guiding around the world. It is an orderly and workable system, a cementing of understanding among individuals, and ultimately among nations.

(Top) Guiding on the move, Canadian National Exhibition, 1975. (Left) Brownies take a breather.

(Right) International Camp, Ontario, 1983. (Below)
WAGGGS, delegates Doe Lake, 1972.

"The particular committee to which I belong has an Australian Chairman and members from Denmark, Switzerland, the Sudan, and Turks and Caicos Islands, as well as Canada. We meet in London once a year, and our work is carried on through detailed correspondence. Our London meetings are intense, and we quickly learn each other's strengths and opinions. It is fascinating to see what each of our very diverse members brings, and so unexpected are the contributions that again and again we are impressed with the value of that diversity. For example, at our last meeting, we were discussing the wording of a memo to go out to all member countries. We all passed easily over the word 'women'—all except Awatif from the Sudan, whose dark face was creased with concern. Finally she told us gently that there was no such word in Arabic; it would have to be mothers, sisters, daughters, nieces, aunts, grandmothers. We got the picture and changed 'women' to 'people.'

"And when a small country suggests that the distribution of something can be easily accomplished through a hand-out at National Headquarters, there is a large country present to point out that not all geography lends itself to such blissful solutions. Similarly, that same large country, with well-developed networks of Guiding, communication, and decision-making, is pulled up short when an emerging nation tells us that an oral, in-person presentation will be necessary for those of its members who don't read. The priority placed on having each girl wear a specific uniform is more weighty in Canada than in a country whose first priority is seeing that its members have enough of any kind of clothing to wear at all.

"One feels very humble in the face of the calm acceptance of problems we would view as insurmountable. And through it all shines the indomitable spirit of Guiding—the sharing, the true sisterhood."

101

(Top) Lady Pellatt presenting Badges for War Service Rally at Casa Loma, Toronto, 1915.

Not all Guides are fortunate enough to be selected for international events, although any Guide unit anywhere in the country can organize an independent trip abroad and will always be welcome at any world centre. And not all adult members will have the opportunity to serve on an international level with the Girl Guides of Canada–Guides du Canada.

But events and rallies — provincial, interprovincial, and even international — are held in this country as well. In fact, rallies have always been a favourite way for Guides to get together.

The first great rally was, of course, that of the Boy Scouts at Crystal Palace in London, England, in 1909. The earliest Canadian rallies were held at Casa Loma in Toronto, the home of the first Chief Commissioner, Lady Pellatt.

"One of these [rallies]," wrote Katherine Panabaker in *The Story of the Girl Guides in Ontario*, "took the form of a play presented by the Toronto Guides in the presence of 400 guests, including children of the Protestant Orphans' Home, in a semi-circle facing the castle. One turret was used for a fiddler, the other was hung with gay banners. Besides the play and dancing on the green, there was the crowning of the May Queen. This most important part was based on the Guide Law. Each month during the year a vote had been taken from all members of the company, who wrote on an unsigned ballot the name of the person who, in their opinion, best exemplified the Guide Law, with a reason why they thought so. At the end of the year the girl who was judged to have kept the Law best was crowned with red roses and given a sceptre of lilies, and ruled as May Queen for the ensuing year. This ceremony took place for several years at the site of Casa Loma in among the trees."

In 1957, "to celebrate the centenary of Lord Baden-Powell's birth, a rally was held in Toronto at Maple Leaf Gardens. Plays depicting the forty-seven years of Guiding were enacted. Entitled the 'B-P Pageant,' a vivid and lifetime portrayal of Hyde Park in

London, England, in 1910, showed people in costumes of the times, with an early high-wheeled bicycle and children rolling hoops.''

"A rally I remember very well," says a former Area Commissioner of Grand Falls, Newfoundland, "was the time that Lady B-P visited in 1961. We had the Scouts and Cubs with us at that time, and there were too many of us for the Armoury. So we had to go down to the stadium. At that time we had special trains, and girls came in from all over the country. We had about 1,500 boys and girls to march into the stadium. They all came in with this fabulous march pattern, and they had a horseshoe that was maybe six layers deep. I remember looking it over and breathing a sigh of relief and thinking, well, they're all in, and they're all in some sort of order. Just before Lady B-P spoke, she jumped to her feet, and she said, 'You've been sitting still too long! Run-run-run-run!' And my heart sank right down to my boots as I thought of 1,500 children running in all directions. All I could think was, 'Will we ever get them in or out again?'

103

(Opposite page, left) ''Guiding on the Move''. Canadian National Exhibition, August 1975. (Below) ''Camp chores.''

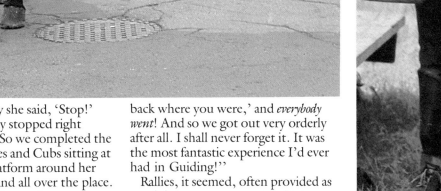

''Then suddenly she said, 'Stop!' And of course they stopped right where they were. So we completed the rally with Brownies and Cubs sitting at the edge of the platform around her and on the floor and all over the place.

''When it was all over, I remember saying, 'Lady B-P, you mixed them up, do you think you could put them back where they came from?' And she just got up and said, 'Everybody go back where you were,' and *everybody went*! And so we got out very orderly after all. I shall never forget it. It was the most fantastic experience I'd ever had in Guiding!''

Rallies, it seemed, often provided as much humour as pageantry. But some of the funniest and most telling stories of girls having just a terrific old time with other girls come from camp memories.

Wref O'Hara, a member of the National Communication and Resource Services Group, has a bearish tale to tell: "One time while backpacking in the mountains, two Guiders were at the end of the column. They were aware of their responsibilities to the group, and had kept well to the rear of any slower, tired hikers. Suddenly, out of the underbrush, a very large bear emerged onto the hiking trail in front of them. This awesome, menacing creature did not seem to mind the tinkling of the bells on their backpacks or the presence of human beings.

"The Guiders' thoughts were immediately of the safety of the group ahead, and then, of course, of their own predicament. What to do? It was, for sure, a bad situation. Looking at each other for moral support, they each at once remembered the Guide Law, 'A Guide smiles and sings, even under difficulty,' and promptly burst into song! The bear was so taken aback by this unusual activity—or was it a critic of harmonious singing?—that it fled back into the wilds.

"It is not known if our two Guiders availed themselves of further instruction in harmony, but they had a wonderful tale for campfire that night!"

"One year I had 200 Guides from Ottawa up at a camp," recounts Betty Russell. "The Quartermaster that year had made a mistake; when she ordered celery from the market, she ordered rather a lot—in fact, she ordered 200 bunches. When they arrived, nobody knew what to do with them. The gardener certainly didn't want to take them back, and so we decided to have a big competition to see who could eat the most celery. I forgot what we told them they could do, but it must have been enticing, because they *all* fell for it, and I swear that every single Girl Guide ate a bunch of celery!"

107

Betty started her Guiding career as a parent in the local association when her daughter was a Brownie. She was encouraged to take on a camping assignment by a very persuasive Guider, Hope Hoey.

"I ended up saying yes, I would go as Quartermaster to her camp, and I spent the next six months wishing I could break a leg or something so that I wouldn't have to go." But once Betty got started, she stayed. She's been Guider to Guides, Rangers, and Cadets; she's been District, Division, and Area Commissioner in Ontario and Quebec; she's been Camp Adviser, Training Commissioner, Provincial Training Commissioner, Provincial Camp Commissioner, and National Programme Commissioner. She obviously enjoyed what she found in Guiding.

"One of the nicest things about being in Guides," she says, "are the friends you make. My very closest friend at the moment is Hope.

"I thoroughly enjoyed the sisterhood of Guiding; it gave me a very good feeling to think that I could talk to other women who believed in the things I believed in and were working towards the same aims."

Working with other women is an inherent part of Guiding. "I remain active because Guiding offers me the opportunity to work with competent and capable women, many of whom have become long-standing friends," says engineer Terry Gillies, Chairman of the National Nominations Committee. "Mine is a male-oriented profession, and although this is changing for women in their twenties, my peers in the business world are still mostly men. Guiding provides a balance, one which I'm sure contributes to my effectiveness in anything I undertake."

"Few youth-oriented organizations have been as successful in promoting a sense of camaraderie and *esprit de corps* among women as the Girl Guides of Canada," observes Her Honour Jeanne Sauvé, Speaker for the House of Commons. "With its programme of shared challenges, responsibility, and service, young girls come to view themselves, and their female companions, as capable, independent individuals, bound together through common interests, ideals, and experiences.

"I am proud to have been associated with Guiding. Many of the friendships made during my years as a Girl Guide at St. Jean Baptist Parish in Ottawa have been maintained to this day.

Guide presented with her Citizenship badge. (Opposite page) Girls representing each level of Guiding pose beside their 70th anniversary crest recreated in flowers in Halifax public gardens.

Although the challenges and responsibilities have expanded over the years, the Guiding ideal of service to my country and fellow man has also persevered.

"As more and more women choose careers outside the traditional roles of homemaker and mother, the need for a comrade with whom they can discuss their concerns and responsibilities from a common perspective gains even greater importance. By instilling such comradeship among its young women, the Guiding movement has made an outstanding contribution in preparing Canadian women to meet the challenges of today with confidence."

WORLD SCOUTING AND GUIDING HISTORY HIGHLIGHTS

1907: Lord Baden-Powell began Boy Scouts in England.

1908: *Scouting for Boys* — the first handbook for Scouting, written by Lord Baden-Powell — was published.

1909: Crystal Palace Boy Scout Rally in London, England. 11,000 boys came, and a small group of girls.
Girl Guides began, under the leadership of Agnes Baden-Powell, the Chief Scout's sister.

1910: Guiding began in Canada, Denmark, Finland, and South Africa.

1911: It spread to Ireland, Holland, and Sweden.

1912: *How Girls Can Help to Build the Empire* — the Handbook for Girl Guides, written by Agnes Baden-Powell–was published, but many Guiders in England and abroad continued to use *Scouting for Boys* as a handbook. Guiding began in the United States and in Poland.

1924: The 1st World Camp was held at Foxlease, England.

1927: The 1st Canadian National Camp held at Victoria, British Columbia.

1928: The World Association of Girl Guides and Girl Scouts (WAGGGS), was established at the Pax Ting International Conference in Hungary.

1939: Second World War
to
1945: The Western Hemisphere Committee formed, as a sub-committee of the World Committee.

1948: The World Conference is held in Cooperstown, New York.

1952: National Camp at Ottawa, Ontario.

1957: International Camp at Doe Lake, Ontario.

1958: All American Camp in New Brunswick.

1961: Guiding Organization in Canada became known as Girl Guides of Canada–Guides du Canada.

1962: Membership within the Girl Guides of Canada–Guides du Canada was extended to the Guides Catholiques du Canada (secteur français).

1967: Canadian National Heritage Camp.

1977: International Camp at Cape Breton, Nova Scotia.

1981: Guiding had spread to 104 countries throughout the World.

PROVINCIAL OFFICES

ALBERTA
200 Tipton Block
10359-82nd Ave.
Edmonton, Alberta
T6E 1Z9
(403) 433-2451

BRITISH COLUMBIA
1462 West 8th Avenue
Vancouver, British Columbia
V6H 1E1
(604) 734-4877

MANITOBA
872 St. James Street
Winnipeg, Manitoba
R3G 2K2
(204) 942-2458

NEW BRUNSWICK
Suite 215, 70 Crown Street
Saint John, New Brunswick
E2L 2X6
(506) 693-3922

NEWFOUNDLAND
Bldg. 566, St. John's Place
Pleasantville, St. John's
Newfoundland
A1A 1S3
(709) 726-1116

NORTHWEST TERRITORIES
Box 2835
Yellowknife, Northwest Territories
X1A 2R2
(403) 873-3138

NOVA SCOTIA
1871 Granville Street
Halifax, Nova Scotia
B3J 1Y1
(902) 423-3735

ONTARIO
50 Merton Street
Toronto, Ontario
M4S 1A3
(416) 487-5281

PRINCE EDWARD ISLAND
100 Upper Prince Street
Charlottetown, Prince Edward Island
C1A 4S3
(902) 894-4936

QUEBEC
1939 Maisonneuve Blvd. West
Montreal, Quebec
H3H 1K3
(514) 933-5839

SASKATCHEWAN
1362A Lorne Street
Regina, Saskatchewan
S4R 2K1
(306) 757-4102

YUKON
Box 5133
Whitehorse, Yukon
Y1A 4S3
(403) 667-2455

GUIDES CATHOLIQUES DU
CANADA
(Secteur Français)
3827 St. Hubert
Montreal, Quebec
H2L 4A4
(514) 524-3753

WORLD ASSOCIATION OF GIRL GUIDES AND GIRL SCOUTS

Argentina
Australia
Austria
Bahamas
Bahrain*
Bangladesh
Barbados
Belgium
Benin, People's Rep. of*
Bolivia
Botswana*
Brazil
Burundi*
Cameroon*
Canada
Central Africa Rep.*
Chile
China, Rep. of
Colombia
Costa Rica*
Cyprus
Denmark
Dominican Rep.*
Ecuador*
Egypt, Arab Rep. of
El Salvador
Ethiopia*
Fiji*
Finland
France
The Gambia*
Germany
Ghana
Greece
Guatemala

Guyana
Haiti
Honduras*
Hong Kong
Iceland
India
Indonesia*
Iran
Ireland
Israel
Italy
Ivory Coast*
Jamaica
Japan
Jordan
Kenya
Korea
Kuwait
Lebanon
Lesotho*
Liberia
Libya
Liechtenstein
Luxembourg
Madagascar*
Malaysia
Malta
Mauritius
Mexico
Monaco
Nepal* ˙
Netherlands
Netherlands,
   Antilles
New Zealand
Nicaragua*

Nigeria
Norway
Pakistan
Panama
Papua New Guinea*
Paraguay
Peru
Phillipines
Portugal
Rwanda*
Senegal*
Sierra Leone
Singapore
South Africa
Spain
Sri Lanka
Sudan
Surinam*
Swaziland*
Sweden
Switzerland
Tanzania
Thailand
Togo*
Trinidad & Tobago
Turkey*
Uganda*
United Kingdom
United States of
   America
Upper Volta*
Uruguay*
Venezuela
Zambia
Zimbabwe

*denotes Associate Members

Girl Guiding/Girl Scouting exists in a number of other countries, with which the World Bureau is in close touch.

Bibliography

PROVINCIAL HISTORIES OF GUIDING

Girl Guides of New Brunswick, 1909–1967. Fredericton: New Brunswick Council of Girl Guides, 1967.

Guiding in Nova Scotia, 1911–1936. Halifax: Nova Scotia Council of Girl Guides, 1935.

Sixty Years and More. Vancouver: British Columbia Council of Girl Guides, 1971.

Cormack, Barbara Villy. *Landmarks*. Edmonton: Alberta Council of Girl Guides, 1967.

Fairley, Lilian. *Guidelines*. Saskatoon: Saskatchewan Council of Girl Guides, 1967.

Fullerton, Jessie R. *The Story of Girl Guiding in Prince Edward Island*. Charlottetown, 1967.

Hutchins, Nancy Bowden. *Guides, All Guides*. Halifax: Nova Scotia Council of Girl Guides, 1977.

Pannabaker, Katherine. *The Story of the Girl Guides in Ontario*. Toronto: Ontario Council of Girl Guides of Canada, 1966.

Wooliams, Edith. *Boots, Tents and Miniskirts*. Calgary: Century Calgary Publications, 1975.

BOOKS

B-P's Outlook (Selections from the Founder's contributions to *The Scouter*, 1909–1941). Ottawa: National Council of Boy Scouts of Canada, 1979.

The Brownie Programme. Toronto: Girl Guides of Canada, 1983.

The Guide Programme. Toronto: Girl Guides of Canada, 1982.

Local Associations. Toronto: Girl Guides of Canada, 1978.

The Pathfinder Programme. Toronto: Girl Guides of Canada, 1981.

Policy Organization and Rules. Toronto: Girl Guides of Canada, 1981.

Baden-Powell of Gilwell, Lord. *Girl Guiding*. London: C. Tinling & Co. Ltd., 1918.

Baden-Powell, Miss Agnes, and Baden-Powell of Gilwell, Lord. *How Girls Can Help to Build up the Empire: The Handbook for Girl Guides*. London: Thomas Nelson and Sons, 1912.

Drewer, Mary. *Window on My Heart: The Autobiography of Lady Baden-Powell*, G/B/E. London: Hodder & Stoughton, 1973.

Queen Margaret School History Committee. *Beyond All Dreams*. Vancouver: Rapier Press Ltd., 1975.

Storrs, Monica. *God's Galloping Girl*. Vancouver: University of B.C. Press, 1979.

PERIODICALS

Alive (Canadian Girl Guide Magazine August 1966–June 1972).

Canadian Guide (1949–July 1966).

Canadian Guider Magazine (1933–present).

Girl Guides' Gazette (London, England, 1914; 1915; Vols. VIII (1921), IX (1922), X (1923); XI (1924); XII (1925).

NEWSPAPERS

The Brandon (Manitoba) *Daily Sun*, Monday, July 17, 1916.

The Canadian and British News (Montreal), January 18, 1913.

Canadian Courier (Toronto), January 14, 1911.

The Evening Telegram (Toronto), August 29, 1912.

The Globe (Toronto), October 1916.

The Mail and Empire (Toronto), 1913.

The Mail and Empire (Toronto), August 23, 1918.

Nanaimo Daily Herald, July 14, 1914.

Owen Sounds, August 6, 1915.

Sherbrooke Daily Record, December 26, 1914.

Toronto Daily News, Monday, October 14, 1912.

Vancouver, B.C., November 1, 1912.

Windsor Evening Record, February 17, 1917.

OTHER

Ashworth, Nesta (1893–1982). "The Crystal Palace Rally". From her unpublished memoirs.

Jarvis, Julia. "The Founding of the Girl Guide Movement in Canada, 1910". *Ontario History*, Vol. 62, no. 4 (December 1970), 213–19.

Design by
Catherine Wilson/Sunkisst Graphics, Toronto

Typeset in Galliard by
Compeer Typographic Services Ltd., Toronto

Text film and colour separations by
D.W. Friesen & Sons Ltd., Altona

Printed and bound by
D.W. Friesen & Sons Ltd., Altona

Jacket printed by
The Carswell Printing Company, Toronto